POET UNDER SATURN
The Tragedy of Verlaine

by MARCEL COULON

Translated and with an Introduction
by Edgell Rickword

KENNIKAT PRESS
Port Washington, N. Y./London

POET UNDER SATURN

First published in 1932
Reissued in 1970 by Kennikat Press
Library of Congress Catalog Card No: 77-103176
SBN 8046-0813-X

Manufactured by Taylor Publishing Company   Dallas, Texas

CONTENTS

CONTENTS

VAGABONDAGE

INTRODUCTION
VERLAINE IN ENGLAND

INTRODUCTION

VERLAINE IN ENGLAND

During the last twenty years French poetry has had a greater influence on English than at any other time, probably, since the Restoration period. If we discount a certain amount of literary snobbery, I think it will be agreed that this influence is justified, for the more recent French poets have shown a keener sense of the requirements of the modern sensibility than our own have, and they have adapted their technique accordingly. We owe them the impulse to directer forms of expression, the contempt for poetry as an "attitude." This tendency originated with Baudelaire and was developed by Verlaine. It is perhaps more than a coincidence that both poets were from their school days familiar with English, and it may be that the intimacy of feeling which the first, and the pure lyricism which the second, restored to French poetry were to some degree learnt from our own poets. Such geographical accidents are not often important, but it does seem likely that Verlaine was encouraged to follow the natural bent of his genius by the example of our Romantic poets.

There are many poets, and the very greatest are among them, whose lives we do not need to know anything about; with whom such knowledge is in fact more confusing than illuminating, so intricate are the relations between the man's actual experience and the created work. But Verlaine does not belong to that category; the origin of almost every poem he wrote can be attributed to some particular circumstance in his life. It is true that his earlier work, that on which his reputation in this country is almost exclusively founded, is ostensibly objective; but as M. Coulon shows in the present volume, its relation to his most intimate feelings is very close. As his genius matured his work became more and more directly personal, so that without a rather detailed knowledge of his life it is impossible really to understand what he is driving at.

His poetry of contrition, though comprehensible to all who have been brought up under the Christian ideology, gains, I think, by a knowledge that this was not hysterical self-flagellation; his profane poems, since they exploit the universal field of physical experience, need no exegesis; and the same may be said of those pure lyrics in which he expresses a mood in its essence, free from all particular considerations of the why and wherefore; but there is a large body of his poetry which is tempered to the elegiac mood, and in such poems there are frequent allusions to definite events and persons and to the temperamental idiosyncracies that brought him to moral and physical disaster, which it is necessary to understand literally. That must be the justification for telling a story sometimes sordid in its details. Less compunction is necessary than in the case of some poets one could name, for Verlaine was definitely not of the type of poet defined by Mr. Bernard Shaw, who speak to themselves and are only overheard by the world. Verlaine had every intention of being heard, and if many of his poems lay bare his heart, not a few of them display an exhibitionism which is all but physical.

Verlaine, a sedentary type, might quite possibly never have reached England but for the influence of the splendid poet and restless traveller who is famous also as a miracle of precocity; for his last work was written before his nineteenth birthday. Rimbaud has often been blamed for Verlaine's misfortunes. He was not primarily responsible for Verlaine's defection from the banner of respectability; that would have happened sooner or later through the incorrigible self-indulgence of his nature; but Rimbaud did precipitate into disaster an existence which might otherwise have suffered only a gradual and sterile degeneration. It is at least arguable that this catastrophe was necessary to raise Verlaine from the level of a good to that of a great poet.

The association of these two poets, whose types of genius were so different and finally inimical to one another, is an event unparalleled in the annals of poetry. At the time of their meeting, Verlaine, with a private income, a small job in the Civil Service, a pretty young wife and an enviable reputation among the younger writers, seemed set for a steady career and the acquisition of fame by the occasional production of slim volumes of verse. But his sensibility demanded continual stimulation, and once the serene happiness which at a distance had seemed the ideal life had been attained, he quickly found it boring and irksome, even.

This malady was a symptom of the absence of any central control. Verlaine was all epidermis. As Zweig says in reference to him: "A soul which lacks ethical authority for self-control must turn with accusation and pleading towards others, towards something outside the self"; and Verlaine can be seen doing that all through his work. His early ideas, convictions rather, were emotional indulgences masked with a superficial intellectualism. It was as much the convention in his youth to be an atheist as it is now for a minor poet to be Anglo-Catholic; we may assume that Verlaine's motives for the adoption of atheism were as personal, as emotional, as his later acceptance of the Faith, and had as much connection with reason. For one thing, atheism released him from the moral discipline of his childhood, and he had not yet perceived the poetic possibilities of remorse. Verlaine's sincerity is not in question; he always had too many emotions to need to counterfeit any, but it must be realised that his adhesion to an idea is no measure of his understanding of it, but only of the degree to which it satisfied him emotionally at a particular moment. So he was quite happy at this moment sharing the Voltairianism, trimmed with a little "scientific" scepticism, which was the mental climate of his generation.

When Rimbaud arrived in Paris, in 1871, at Verlaine's invitation, he was not yet seventeen. Unlike Verlaine, he was in a state of *energetic* denial of accepted moral values and he had freed himself from the controls of childhood only to evolve a morality that was more strenuous, since its provisions were positive, not merely inhibitive. I have not the space to discuss Rimbaud's ideas fully, but the following quotations may help to account for the metaphysical elopement which followed the meeting of the two poets and which played havoc with Verlaine's life. Here are two extracts from a letter to a friend in which Rimbaud expounds his theory of poetics:

I say that one must become a *Seer*, make oneself a *visionary*. The poet becomes a Seer by a vast, prolonged and reasoned derangement of all the senses.

The poet exhausts every form of experience from love to madness, and though the torment is great and social outlawry must result, he becomes finally the repository of the supreme wisdom:

> For he reaches the Unknown!   Since he has culti-
> vated his soul, richer to begin with than any other.
> And even if, maddened, he should end by losing
> consciousness of his visions, he has seen them!
> Though he collapse in his wild career among
> unheard-of and unnameable things, other horrible
> workers will come forward and they will set out
> from the horizon where the other sank down.

This invitation to explore the subconscious has had far-reaching effects on literature, the results of which can hardly be judged yet; but in Rimbaud it was associated with an intense altruism (to be distinguished from humanitarianism), which had a direct influence on his relations with Verlaine:

> The poet is truly the Fire-Stealer.
>   He is responsible for mankind, for the animals
> even; he must make his inventions felt, palpable,
> audible. . .   The poet should define the quantity of
> the unknown coming to consciousness in his age
> in the universal soul; he should give more than the
> formula of his thought, than the notes of his march
> on Progress!   Enormity absorbed by everyone
> becoming the norm, he would be truly a *multiplier of
> progress.* (15th May, 1871.)

The first, and the last, individual Rimbaud was to make himself responsible for, was Verlaine. But before noticing the result and to show that these quotations were not mere boyish rodomontade, we may observe the effect that Rimbaud's arrival in Paris six month's later had on the Parnassian literary group—men who were by no means addicted to these evangelical enthusiasms. I quote from a recently discovered letter from Leon Valade to Emile Blémont, both friends of Verlaine and talented poets:

2nd October, 1871.

You missed a lot by not coming to the dinner of the Affreux-Bonshommes. There, under the auspices of Verlaine, his discoverer and myself, his John the Baptist on the Left Bank, a terrifying poet less than eighteen years old was exhibited, by name Arthur Rimbaud. Large hands, large feet, an absolutely child-like face suitable to a boy of thirteen, with deep blue eyes and a nature that is not so much timid as wild: such is the lad whose imagination, rich in unprecedented powers and perversities, has fascinated or terrified all our friends. "The makings of a splendid preacher!" exclaimed Soury. D'Hervilly said, "Jesus among the Rabbis." Maître declared, "It's the Devil himself," and that led me to this new and improved formula, "The Devil among the Rabbis."

I cannot tell you about our poet's life. I only know that he comes from Charleville with the firm intention of never seeing his birthplace nor his family again. When you come you shall see some of his poems and you can judge. If Fate is not holding in reserve, as often happens, a thunderbolt for him, *it is a genius who has arisen.* This is the calm expression of a judgment I have already had three weeks to consider, not of a moment of dazzlement.

Among the intellectual perversities Valade refers to, Rimbaud's misogyny must have had most effect on the approaching break-up of the Verlaine household. He was not an anti-feminist, but he clearly stated that at present, and largely for historical reasons, Woman was incapable of being an adequate companion for the "horrible workers" in the Unknown. As Verlaine was just discovering his young wife's inadequacy to supply him with that centre he lacked in himself, it is not surprising that he should think he had found the prop he needed in his young friend's genius; nor if Rimbaud, appreciating Verlaine's spontaneous sensitiveness, should have thought he had found an educable comrade, with the spontaneity of the female without the handicap of the sex, and he explicitly states: "I had undertaken, in all sincerity of heart, to restore him to his original condition of a Son of Light."

But finding nothing much to come of their association in Paris except drunkenness and quarrels, what could seem more logical to Verlaine's mind than that *conditions* were at fault, and that the metamorphosis would take place if he were free from the bickering of the literary cenacles and the boredom of his home? So in July 1872 Verlaine made a not very dignified get-away (see page 99), which he describes years afterwards, in terms that show the influence of Rimbaud, as "a proud departure on the quest of love, far away from an existence surrendered to the common-place. . . In fraternal and illustrious company towards all the regions of the physical and moral universe. . ."

After two reckless months in Belgium the poets crossed over to England. The earliest account of their arrival in

B

London is given by Felix Régamy in his essay *Verlaine as a Draughtsman:*

> On the 10th September 1872, in my studio in Langham Street, where I used to be able to work so well and the memory of which suffices to make me love England and its fog, Verlaine turned up. He had come from Brussels. He was his usual cheerful self, and though but scantily provided with linen, he did not seem overwhelmed by Fate. We passed some charming hours together.
>
> But he was not alone. A dumb companion accompanied him who was not remarkable for his elegance either.
>
> It was Rimbaud.

Régamy sketches them in the street, Rimbaud slouching along some paces behind Verlaine, a suspicious policeman in the background. Whilst Verlaine mixed eagerly with the Communist refugees, and published a poem (commemorating the victims of the Commune, though ostensibly those of 1832) in the paper they printed in Soho, Rimbaud remained sombre and unsociable, foreseeing the failure of his enterprise. The two poets took a room at 34 Howland Street, off Tottenham Court Road. It was just the quarter to satisfy Verlaine's appetite for the bustle and warmth of life, and several of his poems localise his emotions in these crowded districts of London. Sometimes the effect was gay, as in *Dansons la gigue*, said to have been written in a public-house at the corner of Greek Street and Old Compton Street; sometimes it was sombre, as in this later poem, where the past rears up at him through the fog like a whining animal:

Tout l'affreux passé saute, piaule, miaule, glapit
Dans le brouillard sale et jaune et rose des Sohos
Avec des all rights, et des indeeds, et des hos! hos!

Verlaine is indefatigable in writing amusing trivialities
about London to his friend Lepelletier. He is rather
obsessed by our sanitary arrangements and the sexual
commerce of the West End, but here are some more
general remarks:

> London is less dismal than its reputation; it is true
> that you have to be very inquisitive, like me, to
> discover much amusement here; I find a lot. But
> decent cafés, nix! nix! You have to be content with
> the dirty little holes called French coffee-houses or
> with the places for commercial travellers in Leicester
> Square. No matter; this incredible city is all right;
> black as a crow and noisy as a duck; prudish, with
> every kind of vice flaunting its presence; everlast-
> ingly drunk, in spite of the ridiculous laws against
> drunkenness. Vast, though really it is only a group
> of little scandalmongering towns in rivalry; ugly
> and unimposing, without any *monuments* at all,
> except for its endless docks (which are enough,
> though, for my poetry, which is now more and more
> modernistic . .). The fog begins to show the end of
> its nose, everybody here is coughing except me,
> but then I am all wrapped up in flannel... Grog and
> punch begin their syrupy reign. . .

"I live an entirely intellectual life here," Verlaine
asserts at one moment, though this is hardly borne out
by the evidence. His comments, though more vivacious,
show no greater perception than those of the ordinary

tourist. But one cannot but be amazed by his ability to revel in whatever was offered, however sordid; whilst Rimbaud (as he expressed it in a prose poem), still immersed in his ambitious plunge to the Unknown, "made his way to the window and created, beyond the country traversed by bands of delicate music, phantoms of the nocturnal luxury *to come*."

The best comment on this first visit to England was made by Verlaine himself some twenty years later:

> I crave in all humility to add that my first sojourn in London was of a rather frivolous nature, to use no stronger expression, and that I very nearly lost there entirely that seriousness from which I have since then rarely deviated.

To shorten a story which spread over some nine months, Rimbaud found that he could do little to restore his friend to what he had believed his "original condition"; and Verlaine decided that discipleship to a visionary was even more irksome than married life. He made a rendezvous with his wife in Brussels and when she refused to keep it he became so distraught that he made that attack on Rimbaud for which he spent eighteen months in prison at Mons.

In spite of his frivolity, Verlaine had found time to write a few of the poems in *Romances sans paroles*, and M. Gt.-Jean Aubry, in his valuable essay, *Paul Verlaine et l'Angleterre*, sums up the result of this visit in these favourable terms:

> From "Birds in the Night" to "Beams," the English atmosphere had been far from inclement to Verlaine's poetic genius. It had definitely cut him off

from the Parnassian mythologicalism; it enhanced his directness, helped him to shed the literary manner and to prepare the incomparable instrument he was soon to use to express the murmurs, sobs, cries and prayers of *Sagesse*.

Verlaine arrived in London again in March 1875, two months after his release. This was to be his longest, most productive, and least eventful visit. He applied for a schoolmaster's post through an agency, and after about a week accepted one at Stickney, Lincolnshire; board-and-lodging seems to have been the only remuneration. Verlaine described this period of his life very well in an article he contributed to the *Fortnightly Review* in July 1894. He had been met at the station by the school pony and trap and this is his account of his arrival:

Twilight was about to fall on the scenery in front of us. The last rays of daylight were shedding lustre upon a landscape which was exquisite in its rich sweetness of pasture and trees—those English trees with their branches capriciously twisted and intricated, if I may be allowed the barbarism, which the Bible somewhere says are those that bear the best fruit; both sides of the road, which were fringed with fine quick-set hedges, were studded, so to speak, with big sheep and nimble colts roaming free. I made a sketch of the scene in these few verses, which are taken from my book *Sagesse:*

> L'échelonnement des haies
> Moutonne à l'infini . . .

. . . We found ourselves opposite a gateway. . . It was opened to allow us to enter a yard, probably the playground, by a man in the thirties, with a large moustache and enormous whiskers, whom I could just distinguish in the dusk as he raised his felt hat and greeted me with the words, "Welcome, moussou."

To which I replied as soon as I had alighted, "Excuse me, I have got plenty of dust."

To this rather doubtful English he replied in not less questionable French, "Veux-tu laver?"

"Yes," I said, with an approach to correctness— at least, so I pride myself.

Verlaine came to be on very good terms with his employer, whom he coached in classics in return for help with his English studies, which he followed "from Marlowe to Addison and from Fielding to Macaulay." He seems to have been happy; his pupils did not give him much trouble and he was favourably impressed by the quantities of food. He made the acquaintance of Canon Coltman, who had known Tennyson and was an excellent talker. Commenting on the canon's death, Verlaine says: "I am sure that if there be a God and this God is a Catholic, he must be saved; he was so charitable in addition to his other virtues." A remark that bears out, I think, the suggestion that Verlaine's intellectual sophistication did not go very deep.

In the spring of 1876 his mother joined him and they moved together to Boston, a larger town, where Verlaine hoped to make some money by private lessons and so decrease the drain on their not very large capital. After a stay of "some months" at Boston and a short visit to France, Verlaine found a new job at Bournemouth, which he took up on the 21st or 22nd January 1877. (He himself

says "after Easter," but from his letters this is a slip of
memory.)

> I was engaged for six months to teach French and
> the dead languages by Mr. Remington, a Protestant
> clergyman who had been converted to Catholicism,
> at his small but very select school of St. Aloysius...
> on the top of the high cliffs covered with furze I
> have seen leagues and leagues of sea in every
> direction, even as far as the first rocks off the shores
> of the Norman Islands, and I composed some verses
> in this style:
>
> > La mer est plus belle
> > Que les cathédrales . . .
>
> I also wrote a short poem called "Bournemouth"
> (*Amour*), which has been considered good. How-
> ever, it is too long to quote here.

Verlaine must have stayed at Bournemouth till the
end of the summer term 1877. He was in France in
August, but back in Bournemouth in September, probably to collect his belongings and the "two splendid
certificates" (from Andrews and Remington, presumably)
referred to on page 128 of the present volume, as he had
decided to live in France again. In November 1877 he
was certainly at Rethel, Pas-de-Calais, teaching literature,
history, geography and English. He stayed there till
August 1879, when he returned to England, to Lymington, where he was employed during the Michaelmas term
of that year. It is on this visit that M. Coulon supposes
him to have been accompanied by Lucien Létinois, the
pupil to whom he had become so much attached at
Rethel.

At Lymington Verlaine stayed only the three months of the Michaelmas term. He found the New Forest very charming and used it as a setting for one of his poems. He was recalled, he says,

> by anxiety for his mother's health, "and thus abruptly ended what I have called, with some pomposity, my 'career as a teacher' in England, where I was afterwards twice destined to return, and by and by I propose committing a few notes to paper on the subject of these later visits."

This "twice" is interesting. There is, of course, Verlaine's well-known visit to give lectures over here, and he did write an account of that; but I have not been able to find any trace of the earlier visit (it must have been earlier, for after Lucien's death the series of Verlaine's letters becomes pretty well continuous, and also at that time his movements would have attracted attention). I must refer the reader to page 144, where M. Coulon discusses a statement made by M. Delahaye. It may be that Verlaine's "twice" bears out that statement, in its general sense if not in detail. The only other scrap of information I have been able to find is in a letter relegated to the appendix of the second volume of Verlaine's letters, where, discussing the poem commemorating Lucien's "fault" and confession, he puts in brackets after the word "misdemeanour" (English), which might signify many things, but most plausibly, the geographical position of the sinner. So the mysterious visit may have been connected with that affair.

These lengthy but unexciting reminiscences by Verlaine of his stay in England emphasise that side of him which is referred to, but not very extensively illustrated,

in the following narrative. I mean the real attraction
that a quiet, respectable life had for him. Of course,
his temperament made the continuance of such an existence at best precarious, but it was from the opposition
of these two tendencies that his most poignant emotions
were generated.

Verlaine's last visit to England was accounted for in
this way. Two young admirers of his work, Arthur
Symons and William Rothenstein, had made the poet's
acquaintance in Paris in the early 'nineties, when, in spite
of his reputation, he was never very far from destitution.
Through their efforts and with the help of other English
men of letters enough support was obtained to ensure
the success of a lecture by the poet in London. Verlaine
wrote an account of this visit, and though the original
French has been lost, a translation of it by Arthur Symons
was published in the *Savoy* for April 1896. His letters
show that whilst he was being lionised in London he was
also the protagonist in a most emotional drama, for he
had left two mistresses in Paris and had parted from them
at one of the more intense of the frequent crises in their
relations. These two mistresses were the precious bane
of his last years, for though they bled him without
much mercy they compensated him in other ways—
amply, if we may believe the two volumes of verse he
wrote for them, as no doubt we may; and these joys were
turned into verse and the verse into cash.

He loved both of them in some curious way, and since
he writes to them both as *Chère amie* and addresses the
envelope to Madame Verlaine, it is often impossible to
tell if it is Philomène Boudin, called Esther, or Eugénie
Krantz he is writing to. Apropos of this psychological
phenomenon, I quote from the notes to the late M. Ad.

Van Bever's edition of the poet's letters. Under *Eugénie Krantz* he says:

> . . . Verlaine was very much in love with her. She died, we think, about the end of March 1897, and her death passed unnoticed. Saint-Georges de Bouhélier writes: "No woman appeared less fitted to inspire a heart-rending passion. . . I remember that Paul Verlaine expressed a great passion for a 'delicious' woman, as he kept on saying, 'the only one whom he had ever loved, and who deserved to be loved always and loved well.' And when I enquired this lady's name it was not without astonishment that I learnt from her illustrious lover that it was Mlle. Krantz, a quite common prostitute. As a matter of fact, this strange poet was innocently thrilled by a miniature showing his sweetheart at the time of the Empire, in which she was wearing a white-flowered gown, rendered more magnificent still by the stiff grandeur of a splendid crinoline."

This love for Eugénie was not exclusive, though. Two poems have been published, one to Eugénie beginning: "*Bonne fille simple des rues*" . . . the other to Esther: "*Et toi, tu me charmes aussi*" . . . in which the poet seems to associate the two women in the same homage.

Verlaine arrived at Dieppe on the night of November 19th, 1893, but the weather was so bad that the cross-Channel services were suspended, and all the hotels being full, he was obliged to spend the night on a couch and all next day in the buffet. His state of mind at the time is worth examining, as it is reflected in one of the more interesting of his latest poems. It appears that he

had discarded Eugénie, for the time being, before setting
out for England, in order to concentrate on Esther, to
whom he was more attracted, perhaps because she made
him suffer more, through jealousy; though Eugénie was
a tartar in her own way, and even tore up some of his
manuscripts. At any rate, at this moment, this child of
fifty imagined himself setting out to cross the boundless
ocean and sack the riches of the Indies for his queen—for
the poem is called "Conquistador" (*Pall Mall Magazine*,
November 1894):

> My heart is swollen as the sea since I am leaving my
> beloved one, swollen and bitter as the sea.

> The sea that I must cross, with brave heart and calm
> mind, though I am banishing myself from my queen.
> I embark amidst the tempest in anxious expectation
> of the treasure I am in quest of;

> To bring it back joyfully to her, gold, silver,
> pearl and diamonds, with my heart thrown in. . .

Then, lulled by the swell, he falls asleep:

> Dreaming of infinite corridors filled with heaps
> of gold for my sovereign . . .

He reached Victoria about two o'clock in the morning
and took a cab to Arthur Symons's address in the
Temple, admiring the appearance of the city in the calm
moonlight. He found his host anxiously awaiting him,
after several fruitless visits to the station, at the porter's
lodge:

> ". . . we talked, for two good hours, about every-
> thing under the sun, Paris, poetry, money, too
> (poets think of nothing else, and with reason!), my

future lectures, and ate an entire box, one of those long, tall tin boxes of tea-biscuits (muffins, in English (1)), washed down with plenty of gin and soda (2) and perfumed with vague cigarettes. And it was, I assure you, one of the best and gayest meals I ever had in my life."

(1) They were Osborne biscuits.—Ed. *Savoy*.
(2) There was no soda.—Ed. *Savoy*.

In the morning Edmund Gosse came to take him to lunch, and in the evening he gave his lecture in Barnard's Inn Hall, the antiquity of which inspired him to a poem, as Symons's charmingly situated chambers in Fountain Court had also done. He goes on:

"I, *chétif trouvère de Paris*, intimidated by the imposing place and the rude majesty of the furniture, but encouraged by the numerous and very select audience, installed myself as best I could in the immense chair, at the immense table, and unfolding a roll of notes expressed myself somewhat as follows . . ."

This lecture, like those he had previously given in Holland and Belgium, consisted of a sympathetic but rather perfunctory survey of the state of contemporary French poetry, followed by an exposition of the graph of Pauvre Lélian's poetic career, which was the real business of the evening. This shows that, however much he may have been at the mercy of life as a man, as a poet he was perfectly aware of the æsthetic metal that could be smelted out of each particular vein of emotional ore this haphazard miner chanced to strike. As the process may be observed in the body of this volume I will not repeat it here.

"Next day," he says, "I was off to Oxford, where I lunched with my friend Rothenstein, in company with the distinguished professor, York Powell (who had done much to further the appreciation of Verlaine's poetry in England). Then with the aid of hansoms we were able to see some of the town . . . unique in its medieval majesty, its buildings, colleges, churches of the good period (I refer neither to our century nor to the two and a half centuries before it)."

Rimbaud's maxim *Il faut être absolument moderne* had fallen on barren ground. As a matter of fact, though, these historical nostalgias that Verlaine felt were as superficial as his modernistic leanings under Rimbaud's tutelage. In the region of the sensibility he exploited, past and present and future only meant the happiness he had lost, the pleasure of the moment and its hoped-for continuance.

But under this unruffled surface love's cross-currents and the financial stresses played out a pretty comedy. On his arrival in Oxford, Verlaine had written to Esther asking her advice on a proposal that he should give a lecture in Manchester, which, though it meant prolonging the agony of separation, would also mean an increase of some hundreds of francs in their common purse. On his return to London two days later he was even anxious for marriage :

As for the bracelet, etc., if it is possible I will satisfy your dear wish. As to marriage, if you are speaking seriously, you would give me the greatest pleasure of my life, and we will go before M. le Maire whenever you like. Besides, it is the best means of assuring something for you after my death. Oh, darling, yes, really, that is still my desire. I love only you, and how much!

I am leading a swell life here, for nothing, gratis. Terrific dinners, theatres, music-halls. But I don't enjoy it much, and I would infinitely prefer to be with my Philomène, even when she is naughty, which does happen . . . sometimes.

And I am not drinking, and I will not drink any more, if my darling forbids me . . . nicely.

On sending his mistress twenty-five francs he remarks that he cannot give her any more as the money is being kept by someone else, for prudence sake. In fact, a gentle discipline was exercised over him whilst in London, though it is said that he did escape for a day or two with a ·pocket full of money, and returned to the "frivolousness" of that first visit. But, at any rate, he reassured Philomène:

Do not be afraid about women. Besides, London was unlucky to me* twenty years ago, on that score. And, then, I love you too much.

And as he goes on we see that a serpent had been lurking in this seemingly idyllic scene.

And you, be good, and no anarchy in our little household, which went so smoothly before; you so happy, queen, and I earning money for you, for you, and not for others, notice! . . . How hard it is to be away from you, jealous as I am!

The same day, fearing the worst and determined to have some defence on his return against the solitude he

*Is this romancing on Verlaine's part, or has it any reference to the poem "Pourtant j'aime Kate et ses jolis yeux," of *Romances sans paroles*, 1874?

hated, he wrote to Eugénie for the first time since he had landed, making up their quarrel, admitting his love for Philomène, but hinting that if Eugénie were agreeable he would settle down with her on his return.

With the conspiracy in this state he left London to give his lecture at Salford, Manchester, where he was the guest of a Congregational minister, surely a peculiar conjunction. Two days after his return to London the storm broke, and he wrote Philomène this letter:

> It is in the depths of despair I write you this. When a fixed idea seizes a man, all is over. I have a suspicion, everything tells me, the past, the present, three thousand francs spent or put away without any advantage to me, the things people say,— everything indicates that you have a lover, that you are living with him and that he is making a fool of me, as he is of you. At your age one does not have a lover of twenty-nine for nothing! . . .
>
> . . . and you want me to trust you with all my money. Thanks! and —— to the pimps who would lick their chops over it. . .
>
> All the same, I love you too much—for one can love without having trust—to give you up.

The same day Verlaine wrote to his publisher, warning him not to let anyone, not even Philomène, draw on the money he had sent him for safety from London. He mentions that he is to give his last lecture in London that night. The "infinite corridors filled with heaps of gold" have shrunk to this: "less money than I expected."

The following day Verlaine wrote two letters, one to Eugénie:

I am going to part from Esther, though I am very sorry to. I love and always shall love that woman. But she is dangerous to me, and my resolution is best. You have always been good to me, and it is only with you that I work well. Never speak to me of the other one again. Be better tempered and all will go well.

Till to-morrow, and we will have a nice little dinner, near the station, before going to by-by.

To Philomène he wrote:

Good-bye, then; it is better so. When you have need of me, let me know and I will do anything. But to live together, that's impossible. You will always be paying young men.

So it seems that Eugénie claimed the conquistador's spoils, but one cannot be sure. I wonder how many of Verlaine's distinguished and respectable audience—"select" as he characteristically calls them, would have sympathised with these inner conflicts of the poet they were petting!

Then all too soon the time came for me to leave England, and after some days of delightful dawdling through London, of theatres (a very fairyland), music-halls (a very paradise!), of good and excellent visits received and returned; after having shaken so many really friendly hands, William Rothenstein, Arthur Symons, Herbert Horne, Edmund Gosse, John Lane, William Heinemann, Frank Harris. . . I embarked once more, this time on a sea as still as glass, happy, certainly, at the thought of seeing France again, but very happy, too, at the thought of so agreeable a visit and of such good and enduring memories!

He returned to Paris by the Calais route, as we learn from this curious—his only known attempt at English verse—fragment scribbled on a piece of note-paper stamped with the address of one of his recent hosts:

IN THE REFRESHMENT ROOM

I'm bored immensely
In this buffet of Calais,
Supposing to be, me, your lover
Loved,—if, true?—you are please.
To weep in my absence
(*blot*) . . . aggravated a telegram
Tiresome where I count and count
My own bores for your sake.
But what is morrow to me?
I start to-morrow to London
For your sake, and then, suddenly,
That sadness, so heavy, falls down.

P. V.

Of course he was not going to, but coming from, London. One can only suppose that this was an attempt to write back into the mood in which he had set out. The lines show, like a number of his letters, that though his taste for our idiom was keen, his control of it was by no means certain.

That was the end of Verlaine's long connection with England, though he kept in touch with the friends he names. He died two years after this visit, and in the interval his letters refer to the manuscripts his friends

c

were trying to place for him in English periodicals. A fragment of a note to William Heinemann seems to recall the sentimental episode noticed in the footnote to page 30:

> As to the short poem I am sending you, it was written about a little girl, "a little devil," and naturally very nice; not without an allusion to an adventure which goes ·back to the time shortly after the publication of *La Bonne Chanson*, i.e. 1872.

That was the last echo of Verlaine's first visit to London, a momentous one for both the poets concerned, for if it helped to make Verlaine a great poet, it certainly contributed to Rimbaud's irrevocable decision to abandon poetry.

To say that if Verlaine had not been a poet he would have made no impression on his age, is not extravagant, I think; though it is almost unique in a poet of his rank. For with most other poets we feel that their quality of mind must have distinguished them in some other way if they had not possessed the poetic gift. We have only to compare his letters with those of Keats or his prose remains with those of Baudelaire to realise that he had no real philosophic interests. He was a shrewd observer of men and things as they touched him; he was no fool, that is to say: when he deals with generalities he appears a simpleton because his mind could not deal with experience in that way. It was to his advantage as a poet that he could not rationalise an emotion, did not see it in relation to other emotions of more and less importance, as poets who have not Verlaine's emotional spontaneity or innocence must do. A scheme of things that gave significance to his suffering was all he needed, and his conversion was certainly, among other things, a great piece of æsthetic strategy. Though he never slackened in his admiration for Rimbaud, which was as nearly intellectual as anything he ever felt, and which is magnificently expressed in the poem "Crimen amoris," where he attributes to Rimbaud the challenge:

Oh! je serai celui-là qui créera Dieu,

he soon retired from the attempt, useless ...or him, to invade such advanced regions of metaphysical speculation.

To discover Verlaine's poetry, at however early an age, is not to be irremediably changed in mind, as one might be by Baudelaire or by Donne. He accepts, as most men do, what life brings him, and knowing what it did bring him, one sees that nothing could be more mistaken than to regard him as morbid, and as a decadent poet. The romantic cry; "Anywhere, anywhere out of the world," would have left him cold, even in his moments of greatest distress, I think. And if one of the least disputable definitions of classic poetry is that which differentiates it from the poetry of day-dreams, that which attaches it to poetry dealing with actual experience, and, by implication, with a tendency to the commonplaces of experience, then Verlaine is decidedly the classic poet of his age.

Verlaine's work has been generously praised by a succession of critics from Arthur Symons to Harold Nicolson, but Marcel Coulon's study, with its fresh material and independent views, is supplementary to those others. It should extend the appreciation of Verlaine's poetry by reminding us that the range of his work is a good deal wider than is illustrated by the usual popular selections from it; and also by insisting that its constant emotional realism is no less vital to the greatness of that poetry than its melodiousness and the delicately imaginative shapes in which it is cast.

EDGELL RICKWORD.

A BORN BOURGEIOS

I.   A BORN BOURGEOIS

To define Bohemian life as the opposite of the life of the respectable well-to-do, is to give the most general yet the most exact description of it. But almost all the great French poets have lived the bourgeois life (though one or two, such as La Fontaine or Baudelaire, have been exceptions for a part of their lives, a more or less lengthy, a more or less happy or tragic part), and Bohemia can really claim as completely its own only Verlaine and Villon. For as for Rimbaud, he eludes classification in this as in all other things—in his Bohemianism, in his poetry, in his psychology, he was a unique creature. The comparison of Verlaine with Villon, so often made, is legitimate, then, though there were wide differences between the two cases. Villon never broke away from the respectable, middle-class life . . . because he never belonged to it; but Verlaine is most distinctly a bourgeois by birth, education, tastes and by his early career. In order to understand what befell him, the first thing to do is to point out how clearly his ancestry stamps him of the bourgeois class.

It may be seen in the first place in his father, who held the rank of Capitaine-adjudant-major when his son was born at Metz on March 30th, 1844. The military career of Nicolas-Auguste Verlaine was as unadventurous as can possibly be imagined for the period. He was born on March 24th, 1798 at Bertrix (then in the Département des Forêts, now the Grand-Duchy of Luxembourg), not

39

many miles from Sedan, and he was born, of all things, a solicitor's son (Note 1).

His full record of service, which, I believe, has never been made public before, is given in the notes (Note 2), and here are the essential facts. He enlisted as a volunteer in 1814, when he was sixteen, in an Engineer regiment, and was steadily promoted till he reached the rank of senior captain in 1844; he retired in 1848. In 1823 he was on active service for the first time, at least as far as his papers show, being attached for nine months to the Second Corps of the Army of Spain. From 1825-8 he was with the Army of Occupation of Cadiz, and 1830-1, with the Army of Africa. The archives of the War Office inform us that he was "present at the siege of Cadiz and the attack on the Trocadero, where he distinguished himself."

With all that, he certainly deserved to be decorated Chevalier of the First Class in the Royal and Military Order of Ferdinand of Spain in 1829, and in 1830, Chevalier of the Legion of Honour, but there was nothing to indicate that he should beget a son so subject to the malignant influence of Saturn as the author of the *Poèmes saturniens*.

On his mother's side Verlaine's descent seemed no less reassuring, no less likely to ensure that he would remain what he was born, that is to say, "a perfect *petit-bourgeois*, a sanely balanced man if there ever was one," as he was to write in his *Confessions*. Elizabeth-Stéphanie-Julie-Josèphe Dehée, his mother, was born on March 23rd, 1809, at Fampoux. She was the daughter of a farmer whose father was already of independent means, and the marriage of the parents-to-be of the poet, at the Hôtel de Ville, Arras, on 15th December, 1831, was as thoroughly bourgeois on the bride's side as on the bridegroom's. Between the birth of Paul Verlaine and his reaching manhood the two families, the one in their native Pas-de-Calais, the other in their Ardennes, continued to push out roots into the fat soil of this social stratum. And it was with them, with the Dehées of Fampoux, independent or merchants; with the Dujardins of Lécluse, sugar manufacturers (one of Madame Verlaine's sisters married a Dujardin); with his aunt Grandjean, his father's sister and widow of a colonel at Paliseul, near Bertrix, that Paul passed many comfortable and pampered holidays before his marriage.

If his father left the army—after thirty-three years, eleven months and eleven days in the harness of a bureaucrat rather than a warrior—and Metz, to settle in Paris, it was because he was discontented about some matter of promotion in which he thought himself unfairly treated, as we are told by Lepelletier, who was the poet's friend from school-days and is his principal biographer. Another reason, too, no doubt, was the fact that the family had at their disposal what was a more than average fortune for that period. Lepelletier, whose father, as legal representative of a great banking house, would have been in a position to judge their financial position, estimated it at four hundred thousand francs.

By the time our capitalist died, on December 30th, 1865, a considerable proportion of his capital had been swallowed up by unlucky speculations, but he none the less left his widow and son in easy circumstances, particularly as the latter, then nearly twenty-two years old, had been employed at the Hôtel de Ville for eighteen months past.

Lepelletier says:

M. Verlaine, the father, whom I knew, was a tall
old man, spare and upright, with a thin face, tanned
and withered, and a short, white moustache. His
expression was generally stern, but not ill-tempered
... He adored his son, though he treated him rather
severely, particularly in appearance. He would have
liked to spoil his son, but made himself something
of a bogy on purpose. He used to call every day
at Landry's boarding-school, in the Rue Chaptal,
to enquire after his son's health and find out how
he was getting on with his lessons, and he always
brought him some tit-bit from last evening's dinner,
put aside especially for him. .. His mother was a
tallish woman, thin, upright, slim-waisted, with a
dignified bearing; in general she was aloof and calm
... She worshipped her Paul, spoilt him and forgave him everything (Note 3).

Such conditions were very different from those that
fell to the lot of François Montcorbier:

> Poor I have been from my youth,
> Of poor and humble birth.
> My father never had much money,
> Nor his father, named Horace.
> Poverty followed on the heels of us all.

As for this father of Villon, what was he? What was his
moral influence, if as far as money was concerned he
hardly counted? Was he simply the legal father of a son
who seems never to have known him and who did not
take his name? And what was the poet's mother, before
she comes on the scene in her old age, "destitute and
decrepit" and quite illiterate, adoring the Holy Virgin,

"for fear of Hell, where the damned are broiled"? What ties attached him to the churchman who, lifting the child out of the gutter, sent him to the Sorbonne to prepare him for taking orders? From this Maître Guilluame de Villon the author of the *Grand Testament* received benefits that would have sufficed—had such been his destiny— to ensure him an honourable and comfortable living; but he imbibed along with them, coming as they did after a childhood of poverty and the influence, perhaps, of what is now called a tainted heredity, those anti-social ferments that were to turn him into a downright rogue.

Verlaine, however, was to retain from his family, from his education, from his favoured start in life, first an indisputable probity and then a profound respect for this established order of things against which François Villon kicked so hard. The Bohemian Verlaine, who was sometimes nearer in appearance to a tramp than to a Bohemian, was always to remain on the right side of that boundary that separates the upright citizen from the criminal. Like Adam and Eve banished from Paradise, he and his Muse will deplore, even amid their wildest follies, the loss of that Eden at the gate of which the archangel we call "policeman" stands guard. "Your new profession, the noblest of all after the vocation of the priest and the function of the magistrate," writes this curious father, for the benefit of his son, when he shall have reached the age for military service, in his *Voyage en France par un Français*,—a catechism of ultra-conservatism so extreme in its views that it makes one a Bolshevik, at any rate whilst reading it, which does not take long. The echoes of this conservatism persist less irritatingly in the prose of his later years, when he was so profoundly Bohemianised, and in his *Confessions*, a con-

trite account of how he came to forfeit his bourgeois
status; and also in subjects lending themselves so little
to civic loyalism as *Mes Prisons, Mes Hôpitaux*. What
would a writer less fundamentally bourgeois have made
of them! Though far from heróic, except on paper
(though it is possible to be incapable of heroism whilst
yet remaining a true patriot), he will give us more than
one poem in praise of the flag, as well as his *Ode à Metz*.
And is it not curious to compare the patriotism of a
citizen so shorn of worldly goods as Verlaine, with the
defeatism of a member of the possessing-class so snugly
lodged as Anatole France? Such is the way of the world!
. . . Finally, this grouser who never ceased to blame his
wife for his misfortunes, with the most monumental
injustice, yet will declare that, socially, he got no more
than his deserts:

> And why, Society, since I have offended your rigid
> laws, why should you pamper me?*

And a further reason for this submissiveness is, that a
pretext is necessary even for the most gratuitous recri-
mination. The wolf in the fable needed pretexts for
devouring the lamb, and Verlaine could produce them
against Mathilde Mauté, his wife; but against society all
excuses were lacking. And if in writing these lines in
Sagesse, Verlaine is not addressing himself, as is generally
thought, but actually Rimbaud, none the less we would
turn the apostrophe against him if he deserved it:

> Wretch! every good gift, the glory of baptism, your
> Christian upbringing, a mother's love, strength and

*In a poem describing his daily walk with other prisoners round the exercise-yard in Mons prison. (T)

health like bread and water and lastly that future
which was as surely announced in the picture of that
past as the succession of the tides . . . you ravage
and waste it all. . .

But Verlaine does not deserve that we should, for what
he says here to his one-time companion-in-hell he never
ceased to repeat to himself.

WHOLLY SENSUAL

II. WHOLLY SENSUAL

I. DRINK

We would have turned those lines just quoted against
Verlaine if it had been our business here to moralise.
But our concern is analysis, and if it did become us to
moralise, it would not be to condemn but to absolve.
No more than Villon, no more than Rimbaud, did
Verlaine deserve his destiny. In the psychologist's eyes
no one deserves his destiny; to blame the criminal seems
to him as superfluous a task as to laud the saint; the one is
no more responsible for his vices than the other for his
virtues; the elements that compose sugar might have
made vitriol if their nature had worked that way . . .
which does not mean that when we return from psychology to everyday life we have to regard vitriol as moral
and use it instead of sugar. . . But our object is to
explain why Verlaine was Verlaine and why, when all
the circumstances seemed to head him off from the
Bohemian life, he was fated to sink over head and ears
in it.

Heredity? There is nothing to permit of this explanation here; his ancestors, Flemish or Ardennaisian, seem
to have been healthy and steady men. From all that we
know of the captain, his father, we must conclude that
the poet could not have received his predisposition to
alcohol from him. Lepelletier, who devotes so much
attention to the early signs and development of this

pernicious drunkenness, would not have been backward
in putting the blame on the father, and if he says nothing
we must conclude that there was actually nothing to be
said on that score. Nicolas-Auguste Verlaine is not open
to the same suspicions as the progenitor of Arthur
Rimbaud, an officer, too, but one who wandered from
garrison to garrison and who was for many years in
charge of an Arab station; and it may be remarked that
under the Second Empire *bureau arabe* was the slang name
for the absinthes that later became known as *bien tassés*,
or, as we might say, "stiff ones."

Education? No child was ever more prudently brought
up than Verlaine, no boy more carefully guided to manhood. A firm and kind discipline—a firmness necessitated, we may be sure, by certain signs his father could
perceive—controlled the future poet. And we may see
what fruits it bore in the certificate that the poet attached
to his application for a post in the Hôtel de Ville. This
certificate was given him by the headmaster of the
Institution Landry, where the poet was a boarder, and
within reach all the time of his parents' effective supervision, from 1853 till July 1862 ; and during the same
period he was attending the lectures at the Lycée Bonaparte (now the Condorcet), from the lowest to the matriculation class. This certificate places him amongst the
school's most distinguished pupils and enumerates the
scholastic triumphs on which Lepelletier dwells in detail.
But although Verlaine had matriculated, his father was
not going to let him rest at that. After a three months'
holiday with the Dujardin's at Lécluse, the young man
obtained a post with an insurance company whilst he
read for a Civil Service examination, in which he was
successful. In March 1864, he became a copying-clerk

PAUL VERLAINE

At the age of fifteen, by a college friend.

at the Mairie of the IX arrondissement, and was soon
transferred to the Hôtel de Ville itself, where he was
attached to the pay office.

What would have happened to this "big child," as it
is customary to call him, and we will not fail to conform
to custom (for an adult does remain a child when he
cannot dispense with guidance, when he is as incapable
of managing his own life as a child is of walking alone
in the street), what would have happened if his father
had been spared to him for a few years more? . . . I
cannot say, but at least, by the time he lost his father's
controlling influence he was himself a man, and all
possible precautions had been taken. Shall we regret,
then, that he found his mother excessively indulgent to
the first glaring manifestations of the first of the two
vices by which we shall begin to explain his fate?

> She adored her Paul, Lepelletier says, spoilt him and
> forgave him everything. She did not dare to chide
> him when he came home drunk, which was pretty
> often. She helped him to go to bed, looked after
> him, brought him sugar-water and herb tea; then
> she would go to her own room and weep. But
> next morning she was always full of indulgent
> words to hearten her dear drunkard, to excuse him,
> and to throw on his companions (of whom I was
> one) the blame for the excessive drinking to which
> he gave way quite spontaneously, in full freedom,
> without being pressed and without being induced
> to do so by his friends' example, for we were a
> long way from drinking to the extent he did. One
> or two of our friends were, on the contrary, exces-
> sively abstemious. L. Xavier de Ricard drank noth-

ing but water; Coppée and Dierx went to the café
only to meet and to talk.

Ought his mother, then, her husband gone—this
mother who was not to leave her son until his marriage,
and when that was ruined, not again till her own death,
and through what years of Calvary!—ought this mother
of sorrows to have been capable of taking her husband's
place? Ought Elisa Dehée to have possessed some particle of the authoritativeness with which Vitalie Cuif,
mother of the author of *Bateau ivre*, was too plentifully
endowed? Rimbaud, fatherless like Villon, had too
much of the strap, and Verlaine not enough! . . . Leaving
Rimbaud aside, the explanation will not fit Verlaine's
case. By the time he was free of all authority but his
mother's, the author of *Poèmes saturniens* was beyond the
reach of any help from authority of the family or moral
order. For he was already under the domination of
drunkenness in the full sense of the term, and he had
committed himself to it long before losing his father.

Why was Xavier de Ricard a sober man? Why did
not the demon of alcohol seize on Coppée, Dierx or
Lepelletier? Why did it attack Verlaine the moment he
left school? For when he returned from that first holiday
after his matriculation he was already a "boozer." Such
was the effect of those country liquors whose local names
he tells us in the chapter of his *Confessions* devoted to the
admission of his "rage for drinking,"—*de l'breune et de
che blinque et du g'nief, sans compter les bistouilles*—amusing
words, but serious things for the system, even of a man
of twenty, and dangerous to a temperament already in a
state of excitation. And elsewhere he records the deplorable result, after three months of the Artois village fairs,

of some weeks of " 'sittings' in the low bars in the rue
Soufflot," made possible by his first, and only, term at the
neighbouring Ecole de Droit.

An hereditary alcoholic he was not, but the disease
may be contracted, too, it seems, and without there being
any more inherited tendency to it than to tuberculosis or
to syphilis. But if, none the less, one insists that his
alcoholism can only be accounted for by some organic
predisposition, then Verlaine has referred to this many
times by its true name, attributing all his faults to it.
And it is perfectly true that, had it not been for *Sensuality*,
he would have made the best son in the world, and so,
too, the best husband, father and citizen,

> Bad, yes, but not wicked. Sensuality alone, the
> flesh wild from loins to lips, disturbed his holy
> desires.
> The beauty of bodies and eyes, scents, feasts,
> intoxications, caresses and indolences, only these
> barred the way to heaven.

Verlaine was a reveller in every kind of pleasure, in
the material as in the spiritual, in the subtle as in the
gross; to him none came amiss, he found them all
delectable. With a mad ardour for whatever could satisfy
the palate and the loins, as for all that could satisfy the
emotions and the mind, he rushed to alcohol as he was
to rush to friendship, as he rushed to love, to art and to
God, without deliberation and without restraint, a
glutton spurred on by an epicure. Those who never
saw him, as I did in the winter of 1892, reciting a poem
by Hugo whilst he was tucking into a dish of roast
turkey and chestnuts, can hardly have any idea of the
extreme of pleasure to be derived from eating and from

fine poetry. As regards the latter, I have never seen
anyone more visibly possessed by it, though it should be
pointed out that the poem (*Les Tronçons du Serpent*, from
Les Orientales) was really a *poème saturnien* by anticipation
and that Verlaine was applying it to his own destiny:

> And on the sand I saw the green and yellow snake,
> flecked with black stains. The axe had cut its living
> body in a score of pieces that the waves now lap.
>   That axe's blow crushed, too, the soaring flight
> of your youth, your life and your thoughts. . .

And as for the pleasure of drinking, we cannot believe, in
spite of his protestations, we who have seen him, and
not once only, at the café, that he ever ceased to love it for
its own sake:

> If I drink it is to get drunk, and not for the sake of
> drinking,

he will exclaim towards the end of his life, having then
undeniably many troubles to drown in his absinthe. But
when he first took to drink, about his eighteenth year,
he had no other reason for it than this, that he was
thirsty. He was thirsty, and he found it pleasant to drink.
The line from "La Bonne Chanson":

> the oblivion I sought in accursed liquors

could have been true to his state of mind when it was
written, in 1869, but not to that of 1862. At the age of
eighteen this piece of "whimsical advice," which he gave
to Raoul Ponchon when he was in his forties, would
have meant nothing to him:

> Drink to forget.
> Brandy's a girl

Who brings you the moon
In her apron.

At eighteen, it was weakness before the force of his
impulse, the violence of his need. A need that was
irresistible, or he would have resisted it, for his upbring-
ing had furnished him with all the necessary defensive
weapons; but of what use are weapons when one cannot
use them?

We may, without denying determinism, admit that a
person is free to act in a variety of ways, when it is a
matter of actions that are strictly personal and do not
infringe the liberties of others—to be sober or not, for
example. To drink or not to drink? The first few times
this question arises for a man, it is in his power to decide
it. A system of motives, for and against, is in equili-
brium; his mechanism, if this mechanism is normal, is
allowed a certain amount of free play. It is for him to
give the final flick towards sobriety or its opposite,
which, acting on one set of motives and not on the
other, will set the act in motion. No one else, in fact, has
any interest in the question; neither the universe nor
his neighbour will obstruct his choice. In 1862, when his
gullet was still virgin, Verlaine had, in principle, the
choice of going or not going into the café; having gone
in, to drink a moderate glass of beer or several glasses of
spirits. Unfortunately, he had this choice only in principle, because his mechanism was abnormal and had not
that margin of free-play granted to a Xavier de Ricard, a
Dierx or a Coppée; for where drink was concerned his
sensual predilection was very intense.

And besides, to be able to exercise free will one
must believe that one's will is free. Men who are en-

dowed at the same time with normal appetites and with what is known as "strong character" have the belief that they are free; and in regard to numerous actions of their daily life this belief, reality or illusion, allows them in practice to act as if they were free. But it is precisely this belief in his freedom that, from a very early age, was lacking in Verlaine; the creative and directing concept behind his first volume, *Poèmes saturniens*, is this: that his will is fettered with predestined chains:

> And those who are born under the sign of that sinister planet Saturn, beloved of necromancers, are, more than all others, the old books of magic say, dogged by misfortune and melancholy. A restless and weak imagination is their's, which brings to nought the efforts of Reason.

Weak, Verlaine's imagination? By no means, the reverse was the case; but it was his will that was weak, when it was not made the ally of his appetites. Throughout his work this warning that he placed in front of his first book will be taken up again and again and developed; several years of grave self-observation had preceded this announcement, for he had conceived it clearly long before he formulated it. At school, even, he had read within himself, deduced from his temperament, "burning as lava," the diagram of his life, that diagram that had been

> . . . planned line by line
> By the logic of a malign Influence.

He read it in himself and others could read it too.

Such, for instance, as the boy who drew the sketches reproduced at the beginning of this chapter, who was

in the same form as Verlaine at the Lycée Bonaparte. A
piece of Latin verse is written on the back of these
sketches, from which we learn that Verlaine already
had the reputation of being a poet:

> Verlaine, who in the divine art of the Muses sur-
> passes us all, teach me, I beseech you, to write good
> verses, to translate Latin into French, to render
> Gallic thoughts in the measures of the Romans. . .
> What genius you have! And how beautiful beyond
> comparison. . . You, recently discovered to be the
> perpetrator of admirable poems. . .

This is serious under its raillery and, knowing the
dates of certain pieces in the *Poèmes saturniens,* we realise
that no great French poet (Rimbaud, the monstrous
prodigy, excepted) was as precocious as Verlaine.

> Since you love painting, too, accept this beautiful
> picture. The accompanying marvel is the gift of a
> dear friend. Alexander's javelin is not flung with a
> cruel intention.

The sender, whose name I know to have been Bou-
daille, may no doubt have had Alexander for a first
name, but his sketches tell us volumes about the men-
tality of Verlaine the schoolboy. I do not mean the one
at the top of the page, for I do not know what the subject, a reference to Florian's fable of the big carp and the
little carp, alludes to. But *The Astronomer who fell into a
Sewer,* is not that a perfect anticipation of the fate in
store for the poet, in whom the most delicate idealism
was amalgamated with the grossest materialism; author
of *Parallèlement* as well as of *Sagesse* and who before singing *La Bonne Chanson* ejaculated *Hombres?* Have we not,

in that telescope levelled on the stars and that cadaverous jowl (*bouche d'ombre*, as old Hugo used to say), a perfect illustration of the famous lines:

> The soul ravished to the seventh heaven,
> The humbler body under the table?

Is there not a crying truth in that grotesque Chinese figure guided by a little devil sitting astride his pigtail? A crying truth in the spirit of the thing, and a crying truth in the features, for here Verlaine may be as easily recognised by his features as by his destiny.

II.   LUST AND UGLINESS

Have the Muses ever had, amongst their greatest favourites, a man as ugly as Verlaine? We were acquainted with him at a time when fame, age, and misfortune had laid an aureole on him; with the pride his renown gave him, his ugliness had a distinction, a nobility; at certain moments a real beauty, that was not of an intellectual order only, lit up his features. Yet when he was young Paul-Marie was grotesquely ugly. On this point, as on the preceding one, Lepelletier insists strongly:

> The first time that he came to my parents' house, with his close-cropped head, his hairless chin, his deep-set eyes, his thick and upturned eyebrows, his mongolian cheek-bones and snub nose, my astonished mother let out a cry that was almost like fright: "Good Heavens," she said to me when he had gone, "your friend looks to me like an orang-outang escaped from the Zoological gardens."

And read the portrait that Lepelletier sketches of him when he had grown a beard and was taking part in a farce called *The Rhinoceros*, words by Lepelletier, music by Charles de Sivry, step-brother of Verlaine's future wife; and she, it would appear, was among the audience at this performance, given in the Montmartre studio of the sculptors Bertaux. And as for his appearance just before his marriage, we can learn what that was simply by turning to the daguerreotype reproduced by his biographer.

Where did the unfortunate man pick up such a physiognomy? His mother and father were not a Venus and Adonis, but at least they had human faces; the captain, judging from a portrait we have of him when he was about forty-five (Note 4), might even pass for having been, not a handsome fellow but a fine man in his prime. Elisa Dehée seems, from the portrait which shows her when she was between twenty and twenty-five, to have been not without charm. And Verlaine derives from both of them, from each he took those characteristics susceptible of being turned to ugliness, and emphasised them. To his father he owes his massive skull, compensated in the latter by the length of the face; from him he got his premature baldness, his bushy eyebrows, which turned sharply upwards at the temples; as for his eyes, puckered, long and slanting, these came to him from his mother. And she, charming as she is shown to be in the print, had noticeably irregular features. Under the cunning arrangement of great masses of high-looped hair, flanked with a knot of curls at each temple, may be divined a dome-shaped head like her son's, and like him, too, she has fleshy nostrils, thick lips, the lower part of the face disproportionately long and the cheeks asymmetrical. And we have, too, a photograph of Paul-Marie taken when he was two or three years old, wearing a *bourrelet*, the round, padded cap then the fashion for the toddlers of Languedoc (for his father was in garrison at Montpellier)—but this babe shows few points of comparison with the classic *bambino* of the Florentine quattrocentists.

Such ugliness in a philistine would have been a serious handicap; in a poet, in so ardent an æsthete, in an imaginative man so eager for beauty and pleasure it became an irremediably damaging influence. To appreciate the effect that Pauvre Lélian's* ugliness had on his destiny we must consider it side by side with the ambitious declaration that opens his earliest work:

> Whilst still a child I went about dreaming of Koh-i-noors, of Persian and Papal sumptuosities, of Heliogabalus and Sardanapalus.

And we must notice, in a poem called "Grotesques" in the same volume, the statement that

> the children stick out their tongues at them and the girls make fun of them,

a statement repeated with greater particularity in this admission in *Sagesse:*

> At twenty a trouble not known before, called amorous desire, caused me to find women beautiful; but they did not find me so,

and which he made once more in a poem in *Bonheur* declaring that

*Verlaine first used this expressive anagram when he wrote an essay on his own poetry for the pamphlet *Poètes maudits*, which contained appreciations of Corbière, Rimbaud and Mallarmé, whose work was then almost unknown.

the women . . . judge him far from spruce, with
clumsy ways and a bit grotesque

—and in considering this evidence it must not be forgotten that we have in Verlaine the most completely
subjective of poets after Villon and Rimbaud, the poet
who is most the biographer and psychologist of his own
life.

We have to estimate the force of a sensuality which
made itself felt even in the first poems, suggesting,
under their delicate, etherealised form, more material,
physiological characteristics. To do this we have only
to place side by side with such outbursts of tenderness
in the manner of Sully-Prudhomme as this:

Oh, the woman with the fondling ways that re-
kindle love; the dark-haired woman who is gentle,
pensive and never perturbed; and who sometimes
kisses you on the brow, like a child:

or that unforgettable line:

The tone of dear voices that are stilled,

to place side by side with these the stanzas entitled *Marco*.
This is a poem which is hardly ever read, which is never
quoted, although so many lines of the *Poèmes saturniens*
are quoted and re-quoted; and this neglect is no doubt
due to the explanatory note attached to it, suggesting
that it is merely an amusing trifle. But these stanzas
reveal, with all frankness, the boy's eroticism, boundless
already as a stream in flood, a volcano in eruption; and
we may search in vain among the Parnassians, his pre-
decessors, for a poem where sensuality is so livingly, so
glowingly, depicted. Before exclaiming in that terrible
sonnet *Luxures:*

> Oh, Flesh! the one fruit to bite into in Earth's orchards, bitter and luscious fruit which spurts against the teeth only of those famished for the only Love—man's mouth or beast's, and the rich dessert of the strong and their joyful meal,

where he sounds a note of brutal sensuality quite foreign to French poetry until then, before that, Verlaine had rhymed *Marco:*

> When Marco passed by, all the young men used to crane forward to look in her eyes, those Sodoms where the fires of love pitilessly burnt up your poor hovel, Oh, cold Friendship! All around swept mystic perfumes wherein the soul, weeping, melted away; enchantment flowed from her auburn tresses and mysterious music from her gown, when Marco passed by.

Verlaine's note says:

> The author wishes to point out that the rhythm and design of this song are borrowed from a poem, "Mignon", contained in M. J-T. de Saint-Germain's volume, *Les Roses de Noël.* He thought it interesting to exploit for the expression of a quite different set of ideas a lyrical form which, though perhaps a little unsophisticated, is always tuneful, even when indifferently handled, and with which its inventor, that pleasing poet, has had a distinct success.

Colourless in its title, its cover, its subjects, its sentiments, its style; in body and soul colourless as the flower that lends it its name, this little, forgotten volume might stand for the very type of lyrical ethereality (Note 5). It is the work of a pleasing—pleasing is exactly the word—

minor composer who was to some extent the inventor,
before Verlaine and after Desbordes-Valmore, of the
romance sans paroles, the song without words. So Verlaine
imitated the rhythm and design of one of his poems but,
placing himself at the antipodes to its author's moral
outlook, instead of its spotless sweetheart, portrays a
courtesan of the most fatally alluring type. The Mignon
of Saint-Germain's song is Goethe's heroine, who had
just been popularised among the masses, in 1867, by the
music of Ambroise Thomas. Verlaine's Marco, too,
owes her existence to a great theatrical success of the
Second Empire, *Les Filles de Marbre* (1853), that stern
drama with which Barrière and Lambert-Thiboust
replied to *La Dame aux Camélias*, reminding the world
that the courtesan is, essentially, heartless. Verlaine, who
was a great lover of the theatre in his youth, fond of
humming popular tunes, would have had on his lips, like
all his generation, the famous air to which Marco danced
and sang in that play, amid the jingling of golden coins.
And he remodelled this girl who was on the whole,
whatever our simple-minded parents may have believed,
not a bad sort (not virtuous, evidently, but not vicious,
either) (Note 6), he re-modelled her according to the
dreams of the hyper-æsthetised satyr he was.

The transformation of Mignon into Marco, that is the
whole story of Verlaine's amorous life; it leads us from
La Bonne Chanson to *Parallèlement*, from *Sagesse* to *Chair*,
picking up on the way his two volumes of privately
published verse. It explains, as far as the fact can be
explained, how the unfortunate man will, without
transition, pass from blameless adoration to bestial rut.
It explains how, having embarked on love with the idea
of lily-white purity (no poet ever used the words:

"chaste," "chastity," "chastely," so often as he), he should have come to wallow in the slime of sadistic pleasure:

> But when Marco loved, like the crimson blood that flows smoking and foaming from a wound; streams of lust welled out from that cruel body that its crime absolves. The torrent burst the banks of the soul, drowning thought and overwhelming everything in its path; it leaped up supple and destructive as flame, and then died down.

Baudelairianism, the reader will remark, and literary imitativeness.   Good Lord! of course the author of *Poèmes saturniens* had read Baudelaire, was impregnated, soaked, rotten with Baudelaire.   But why should he be so, I ask as I did before, and not Xavier de Ricard, Coppée or Dierx even?   It is not, I suppose, because it would have been more difficult for him to be original than for them?   And as to the second accusation, it must be realised that for a temperament which is æsthetic to the degree his was, literature is equivalent to nature, rhetoric to sincerity.   Baudelaire's sincerity, with however much literature it is buttressed, is no longer disputed to-day.   We know that that literature, that rhetoric, are not false at all; and those who believed them to be false did so because they were unaware of the reality of the feelings these express (though we must not confuse sincerity with spontaneity; if one kind of sincerity is instinctive, mechanical, there is another kind, in art particularly, which is willed, acquired, and brought off).   Like Baudelaire, Verlaine made rhetoric out of his flesh and blood; and knowing what his life was, when we hear him say:

I have ruined my life and I know very well that all
the blame is going to be put on me. To that I can
only answer that I truly was born under Saturn,

shall we still want to accuse him of being literary? But
between him and Baudelaire there is a great, a radical,
difference; that which separates a man who is physio-
logically cold, whose sexuality is content with the excur-
sions of the imagination (a Joseph who will abandon his
cloak in the hands of Madame Sabatier), from one who
has a voracious sexual appetite; from a being whose
imagination, though at first idealising, always ended up,
and rapidly, as the obedient slave of the physical impulse.
  So much being clear, let us return to Verlaine the
schoolboy. And knowing, as I learnt from the school-
fellow of his who provided me with the caricatures from
the Lycée Bonaparte, that that aristocratic establishment
did not possess another pupil so negligent of his person
and his clothes as our poet, let us follow the ravages in
his brain . . . and lower down, of the Koh-i-noors and
Persian and Papal sumptuosities of his dreams. We can
observe him, having put his schoolboy Heliogabalus and
Sardanapalus behind him when he left school, living in
the brocade and lace of the Watteau figures who people
his next volume of poems, the *Fêtes galantes;* whilst he
himself attempted a dandyism which only, alas, showed
up his defects. We can observe him picturing himself
as one of those handsome rakes,

> The Richelieux, the Caussades and the Chevaliers
> Faublas,

whom he leads with so much envious affection, in his
early verses, to the conquest of the Ingenues; or, again,

E

as the Incroyable in this *Eventail Directoire* found among his papers after his death:

> Love me, do. I've sighed so much, died so often, plotted so much, just to have you adore me—Od's faith, I have.

Thus we can understand how, under the tension set up by the conflict of such ugliness with so much lust (and his intelligence, of which I will grant him as much as you like, would not compensate him for the first, though it may, unfortunately, have intensified the second), how he came to have, or rather to be possessed by, his other vice, that is, homosexuality. He does not seem to have been predestined to this vice, any more than he was to drunkenness, by a congenital flaw; and this vice was probably even more accidental in origin than the other; its primary and predominant cause being his ugliness.

III. CYTHERA AND SODOM

The author of *Hombres** was not one of those organic inverts whose cases the Kraft-Ebbings and Havelock Ellises refer to as "a congenital perversion of the genital functions"; not one of those unfortunate abnormals (let us call them that, in spite of M. André Gide's assurance— *experto crede!* that they are the true lawful possessors of sexual normality and happiness), who have a horror of, a physical disgust for, Woman; who are as strongly repelled by the *odor di femina* as you or I would be by the scent of the male in rut. Verlaine did not in the least

Hombres: the title refers to the pederastic inspiration of this privately printed volume. (T)

belong to the category of these "purists" (Note 7). No one was better qualified to cherish Eve exclusively than the author of *La Bonne Chanson*, of *Chair*, of that counter-weight to *Hombres*, called *Femmes*, in which he who even in *Hombres* had so far forgotten himself as to say with a detached air:

A woman now and then is rather good form,

chants the palinode to his previous celebration of homosexuality; and asserts:

. . . I am not the man for Gomorrah nor for
Sodom, but for Paphos and for Lesbos.

No one, indeed, each time that the opportunity arrived, was to prostrate himself more "wildly, fanatically," before "the burning bush of woman." Only this opportunity was denied him at the moment when the need first made itself felt, because of that grotesque ugliness we have referred to. Not when he was twenty, but as soon as he had reached puberty, well before he was twenty, the women had found poor Gaspard, as he called himself, wanting in beauty. Whence a timidity in his relations with women, an obstacle, rather, which Lepelletier noticed. But the ogre who still roared at us in his last years:

I am all mad for love! My poor heart is wild,
no matter when, no matter what, no matter where!

was one of those who are not able to wait. A great number of homo-sexuals are people who could not wait. For lack of thrushes, they satisfy themselves with blackbirds, birds which are taken more easily because they themselves, very often, cannot wait either. The idea that this sort of game lets itself be caught with less difficulty than the other is expressed in Verlaine's sodomitic volume, most plainly in a poem which has the significant title *Mille e tre:*

> My lovers do not belong to the wealthy classes, they are labourers from the suburbs or the country. Fifteen or twenty years old, rude-mannered and not over-clean, they are brutal in their strength and rough in their methods. . .

Is not the best game, when one is in such a hurry as Verlaine was, the game which at once puts itself in front of your gun? The advantages which that Nimrod attached to the law of least erotic effort (to which the "bosky woods" lent themselves so well) may be further observed in a poem, nothing of which is quotable, beginning: *You, lads of the fields!*

Where is the proof that Verlaine's heresy was fundamentally accidental? It is written on every page of his work. There is not, if we leave aside the part we have just been discussing—there is not any poetry more *feminist*, erotically speaking, than his. And it does not include a particle of that misogyny so aggressively present in Rimbaud's work, though there, too, it was not congenital, but acquired. On the contrary, Verlaine's work contains everywhere, no less than in *La Bonne Chanson* itself, declarations and demonstrations of orthodoxy of which it is impossible to doubt the sincerity. All this manifest orthodoxy so dazzled the observer that it blinded us to a heresy that, even leaving *Hombres* out of account, Verlaine's work certainly does not conceal from us.

Another proof: the last six or seven years of his life, when he was in a sort of way living under public observation and supervision, were quite obviously sexually orthodox. Why? Because then he had no lack of thrushes. Thrushes of what quality! . . . but that was his affair, not ours; the fact remains that he could come by enough of them to have no need of blackbirds. That is why, seeing him happy in the arms of the old courtesans who inspired *Chansons pour Elle*, and *Odes en son Honneur*, we did not realise what he let slip when drawing up the catalogue of their "marvels":

> We are not the man for learned Sodom when there is Woman!

That is why we accepted Lepelletier's thesis, although the work of that fiery champion of Verlainian orthodoxy is rich in facts that are singularly inimical to his argument. That is why we were unable to see that *Jadis et Naguère* contains, with regard to the relations of Verlaine and Rimbaud, the admission of their common heresy; and that *Parallèlement*, where this heresy is proclaimed and celebrated, without doubt remains even to-day, amongst works that can be published otherwise than privately, the most Corydonian*of them all . That is why we overlooked a poem it contains, at first intended by the poet to close his second volume, and that here he called *La dernière Fête galante:*

> Once and for all, good gentlemen, and you, lovely ladies, let us separate. Enough of this sort of epithalamia, and besides, those pleasures were too mild.

Corydon, by André Gide, is an attempted justification of homosexuality. (T)

Let us separate, I beg you once more. Oh, may our hearts, that then bleated too sheep-like, from this day onwards announce, full-throated, the embarkation for Sodom and Gomorrah!

That is why declarations so frank, so detached from "women whom we despised and the last of the prejudices," as the poems *L'Impénitent, Pierrot gamin, Sur une statue de Ganymède* and *Laeti et errabundi* told us nothing. Nor even the bare-faced attack on "normal loves" launched in the poem *Ces passions* . . . which is not surpassed by any in *Hombres* itself; and in which there is a stanza beginning with the line

And to fulfil their vows, each of them in turn . . .

that I will excuse myself from quoting in full.

With numerous homosexuals who are no more congenitally so than Verlaine, habit becomes a second nature. Once experienced, the heresy becomes fixed and exclusive. It is possible to become so accustomed to a certain diet that the stomach will not digest any other. Such was not the case with Verlaine; although he ate this dish with great avidity every time it came in front of him, yet he digested it with the stomach of an ostrich.

And he took pride in his vice; it pleased him to celebrate, in very good verses, too, its nobility and antiquity—in the opening poem of *Hombres*. Not at all like that droll fellow, M. Gide, by discovering it among Fabre's insects; but by enumerating the great men, from Socrates and Julius Caesar to Shakespeare and Louis II of Bavaria, who have been honoured by it:

Shakespeare, abandoning at once Ophelia, Cordelia,

Desdemona and all their lovely sex, celebrated in
magnificent verse the allelulia of masculine beauty,
—and let the fools storm!

The Valois were mad for the male, and our era when
Europe is so middle-class and so feminised, none
the less admired that Louis of Bavaria, that virgin
king whose high heart beat for love alone.

Since we have mentioned the antiquity of this vice, let
us point out how precocious the poet was in his pede-
rasty. It must not be thought that *Hombres* was a volume
perpetrated just before his death, when he was certainly
orthodox, which would mean that it was purely a work
of imagination intended to raise money. We know that,
though *Femmes* was published in the author's lifetime
(1890), *Hombres* was delayed till he was in his grave; it
was in the last six months of his life that he gave up the
manuscript. A very simple critical examination dispose
of Lepelletier's hypothesis. The majority of Verlaine's
homosexual poems are youthful ones. Their prosody is
Parnassian, even Coppéesque; and not only without
resemblance to the versification of *Odes en son Honneur*
but quite different even from that of the pieces in *Parallèlement* named above. It is at the very moment he loves
that the bird sings; and really it does require an effort of
will to bring one's self to believe these canticles—however repulsive one judges them—a work of the imagination.

The disease by which Pauvre Lélian was attacked is a
youthful disease, like measles or whooping-cough. And
though he draws the conclusion that they militate in
favour "of the perfect innocence of his masculine friendships," Lepelletier provides us with the following facts:

Among the cherished friends who, at various times in his life, inspired very strong feelings in him, I recall first one of his cousins, a Dujardin, from Lécluse, near Arleux (Nord), where Verlaine spent his holidays. It was a very ardent boyish friendship of which he made me his confidant in his letters of September-October 1862, and it was quite different from the really intellectual friendship which was the bond between us. He wrote about his young cousin like a lover praising his sweetheart; and at that period the schoolboy Verlaine still preserved his garb of innocence.

For one of his contemporaries at the Lycée, a frail and melancholy youth, Lucien Viotti, whom he speaks of sadly in his *Mémoires*, he felt a deep affection. . .

It is quite plausible that these friendships remained harmless. The letters which Lepelletier alludes to in the first case have not been preserved for us. But what a preparation for the *mille e tre* of *Hombres*, the day when Verlaine became his own master and, immediately, entrusted the guidance of his life to Alcohol! Alcohol, that is the factor that has a hundred times more responsibility for Verlaine's Bohemianisation than the other practice.

For one may still inhabit the lands of respectability whilst indulging in blackbirds instead of thrushes, but short drinks and long drinks, these it is that subject one inevitably to the power of Saturn.

IV. UNDER THE SIGN OF SATURN

When, at the age of twenty-two, in 1866, Verlaine
published the *Poèmes saturniens,* he was the man we have
just visualised. His moral and intellectual growth was
complete. He had not merely skirted the fringes of existence, he had "lived," and his psychological foundations
were definitively laid down. That is why he gives us,
at the very outset, a work equal in value, or all but
equal, to what are later to be considered his master-
pieces. But to perceive clearly the maturity of his first
work we must get rid of a notion that was put in circu-
lation by, I believe, Jules Lemaître, in a study on which
numerous admirers of Verlaine base their judgment
(though it is a brilliant study if we consider when it
was written)—the idea that the artificial is an important
element in the *Poèmes saturniens.* With Verlaine, as with
Baudelaire, we have to grasp the sincerity, the reality,
of the emotions under the high polish of their poetic
style.

A poet of regret, of remorse, of contrition; but preceding, and following and sometimes accompanying
these states "in parallel," with a delectation in and
flaunting of vice; that is the general aspect of Verlaine.
That is what constitutes his originality: not merely to
have trodden to the end a path that Villon and Baudelaire only opened up, but to have continually turned
aside from this path as if to be able to return to it the
better and to enact the epitaph that Moréas was to carve
for him:

But the dedicated poet falls, he flings himself even
into the lowest depths to gain the peaks.

With the *Poèmes saturniens*, however, we are only at
the stage of regret, and of a discouragement which seeks
in art the refuge later to be demanded of the Faith.
Which seeks it and which found it. The poet is encum-
bered with a past full of faults, such grave faults that
this past irremediably prejudices his future. But he
exploits as an artist this regret which overwhelms him,
and finds a real joy in pinning it down with words. No,
the *Poèmes saturniens* are not sad, and beside the *Fleurs du
Mal* they seem joyful. That is because they reflect the
ardour for life, that delight in living which Verlaine retained throughout his worst misfortunes, that vitality
which echoes faintly even in his shabby swan-songs.

"Throw away this saturnian, orgiastic and melancholy book," Baudelaire advises his too-virtuous rea-
ders. Orgiastic, yes, Verlaine's work might pass for
that; but melancholy, never—the *Poèmes saturniens* apart.
Melancholy is not in Verlaine's nature; it is a plant not
included among his indigenous flora, but the seed of
which he picked up in the garden of the *Fleurs du Mal* and
other flower-beds of romanticism—such as that fine
poem from *Les Orientales* that he declaimed for us before
gluing up his beard with turkey and chestnuts. This fact
is recognized in his *Confessions*, where he says: "I have
never been melancholy in my life"; and we shall find that
the more catastrophes he accumulates the farther he is
from being sad--witness the inimitable bantering tone,
so unexpected yet so natural, of his *Mes Prisons, mes
Hôpitaux*. "A lugubrious monster," André Gill called
Rimbaud; Pauvre Lélian was a happy monster, without
bitterness, without rancour against circumstances, apart
from those connected with his divorce, and in the end
he will give up complaining about that even—and he

would have stopped long before had there not been some
question about certain share-certificates. Why all this
good-humour?   Because of his faculty for material
enjoyment. He was so fond of life, had such a capacity
for enjoying it through every pore, that as soon as the
unpleasantness was over he lost all thought and memory
of it, provided only that he passed a few happy moments
—and the moments when he was holding a pen always
were happy ones.

So, then, we need be only half sorry for him and reserve our full pity for poets who are less easily anæsthc-
tised, like Baudelaire; or who, like the author of *Une
Saison en Enfer*, apply not anæsthetics, but cruel and tor-
menting irritants to themselves! Was he ever really un·
happy, unhappy as you would have been had you undergone his misfortunes? On December 26th, 1872, he was
not only parted from his wife, but had lost him for whom
he had abandoned her—and he was about as capable of
living in solitude as a carp in salt water! On top of this,
he had just been served with the legal documents in his
wife's suit for a separation, the approach of which
terrified him. Suddenly, in a letter to Lepelletier:

> Christmas yesterday!   An even worse Sunday to-
> day, almost as much damned holy nonsense. Yet
> goose is "exqueesite." Stuffed myself with it these
> last few days at some Islander's homes! (with apple
> sauce!)
>
> I am very depressed, though: all alone. Rimbaud
> (whom you do not really know, whom only I know)
> is not here any longer. A frightful blank! The others
> are all alike to me. They're mere riffraff, Q.E.D.,
> and which will be demonstrated. But to hell with it!

Damned holy nonsense. . . The editor of Verlaine's
Correspondance (Volume I, p. 80) prints for this (B) . . .
dieusard, and I will not be less modest than he has been.
But before being converted, the future author of *Sagesse*
was a scatological atheist, and when he wrote the word
Bon Dieu it was not with the letter B. His letter con-
tinues with some remarks on the finer points of English
as it is spoken in Leun'deun. *Spleen* is only used of the
physical organ. Just as there is no such thing as *beef-
steack*, neither is there *pale ale*. . .

> "Water-closet" is terribly indecent. One says (to
> waiters), "Deuble you si . . ."
> "*Inn*" in the sense of a bar, is a solecism. One
> says "public-house," and the keeper of it is called a
> publican. There is no such thing as "Stop!" except
> on the steamers; to the cabbies you say: "Much
> obliged."
> By the way, it seems that my wife has fine larks
> *at their place* every Wednesday. Yet my mother has
> been in great danger lately with erysipelas; and my
> son is still the Mauté's little prisoner.

But for all that, there is melancholy in the *Poèmes
saturniens*. And he caresses this incipient melancholy
which refuses to develop as a young man strokes his first
moustache. And in caressing it he finds excuses for his
disastrous conduct. He presents himself, thanks to his
coming under the sign of Saturn, with a certificate of
irresponsibility which, though it does not console him,
soothes him. And which pledges him (which is what he
needed, since he wants to live, and he has to live with his
vices or not at all) to run headlong into fresh disasters.
There is little poetry that has been so meditated, so

much ruminated on, as the emotional portions of the
Poèmes saturniens; it is a book of youth, and consequently
it has youthful tones in it, but the music of youth is
lacking; the psychological maturity of the book is closer
to that of an old than of a young man. It is because we
cannot believe that it is the work of a young man, and
much of it a good deal earlier than his twentieth year,
that we are tempted to find so much rhetoric and artifi-
ciality in these poems. But if we look at it more closely,
if we find out what sort of man the author was before we
attempt to judge the work, and if we isolate the two
factors that had controlled the poet since the beginning
of his adolescence, we shall find that artifice has little
place in it, that artifice affects the expression of the
emotions only, not their conception. And we shall
realise that no other poet (Rimbaud apart) has shown
such a precocious self-knowledge and so sincerely and
unerringly confessed himself. We shall then accept, as it
must be accepted, literally, the title of the book; and the
Foreword which explains why this title was chosen:

For those who are born under the sign of Saturn. . .

will appear to us as a marvellous example of observation
of both past and present, and of prescience as to the
future.

Yes, we may take all, or almost all, this clear-ringing
metrical coinage for good ready money; the idyllic part
where he dreams of Mignon as well as the tragic and
sadistic part where he extols Marco. We can admire the
descriptive side of the work and we can accept its
æsthetic technique, learnt from Leconte de Lisle. The
fanaticism which impelled this emotional type of man
towards the impassibility of the Parnassians:

To us who chisel words like drinking cups and compose passionate verses, unmoved. . .

will not sound false to our ears, because this æstheticism enables him to restrain his thought and feeling within the bounds of delicacy and discretion. And however laden with eloquence they reach us (with that eloquence of which he will one day assert that *its neck must be wrung*—a recommendation he followed only too well in the products of his later years), we shall refrain from thinking such emotions and images as these declamatory:

My soul to fearful shipwrecks hoists its sails,

or this:

Like a screaming flock of frightened birds, all my memories sweep down on me,

or this, true to the moment as well as prophetic:

And I am carried away on that ill wind which sweeps me hither and thither like a dead leaf! . . .

Did I say that as an auto-psychologist Verlaine is not quite in the same rank as a Villon or a Rimbaud? I correct that error. He wrote nothing in which he did not analyse himself. And his one work which seems to be objective, *Les Fêtes galantes*, is not that a stage-setting for himself in the fancy-dress costume he used to affect? A flight far from his actual ugliness to the beauty he longed to have?

In the same way, *La Bonne Chanson* repudiated what he had just been in favour of what he believed he had become.

MATHILDE'S HUSBAND

III. MATHILDE'S HUSBAND

I. LA BONNE CHANSON

In *La Bonne Chanson*, Verlaine is, primarily, the poet of the time of the betrothal; but he is besides, the poet of repentance, of the hopes that repentance brings and of the undertakings that it involves. Such expressions as these :

> Since dawn is breaking, since sunrise is here, since after having fled from me for so long, hope again bends its flight towards me, calling and imploring it; since all this happiness chooses to be mine . . .

> we have done, now, with dreadful thoughts, we have done with evil dreams . . . and put away from us the oblivion sought in accursed liquors . . .

> For I desire, now that a creature of light . . .

with so many like:

> Yes, I desire to walk upright and calmly through life . . .

> Led by you, I would walk uprightly . . . that shall be my pleasant duty . . . the days of danger are passed; etc., etc.,

down to the final:

> I was following crooked paths . . .

are certainly significant. It is no longer Art, it is not yet God, but it is his bride-to-be he implores to draw him out of the abyss into which his vices have plunged him. His two vices: one of them is openly mentioned, as we have just seen; the other remains implied, but a passage in *Amour* reveals that it was equally influential. This passage is most valuable for our knowledge of Verlaine; it is the only occasion on which, dropping his untenable accusation against his victim:

> You have not been wholly patient, you have not had every tenderness,

he found it possible to acknowledge his marital unworthiness; the only place in which are mentioned together the two weights which made up his heavy handicap for the part of betrothed lover, since the *Confessions* admit only to drunkenness:

> He was brutal, he was a common drunkard, he was a husband such as you come across in the slums. It was good that he had forsaken his first loves, but that in no way excused the violence of his ways.

That passage had to be quoted, that too; beside the "accursed liquors" those "first loves" had to be placed; for what affected Verlaine so deeply at that moment, and what makes him so touching, too, is his way of associating contrition with love, repentance with hope. The unhappy poet, like a shipwrecked man clutching the side of the boat he is being hoisted into, clings to the delightful child,

> In a grey and green tucked dress, with the sweet beauty of sixteen,

whom an unhoped-for and undeserved good-fortune has allotted him. To settle down! . . . The need to settle down never impelled a man more forcibly, and the confidence that marriage would have that effect never flattered one more deliciously.

He would drink no more. His "saintly mother" would no longer have to nurse him through his drinking-bouts, nor ever again, after sleepless nights spent watching for his return, should she find him asleep on his bed with his top-hat crammed on his head. She should no longer pass her days in sighing over the dwindling of their capital—she who could do nothing to prevent it—a dwindling that disquieted him himself. He would drink no more, and he who was not the man for Sodom, no, he would enter Paphos by the honourable door. From being the most incompetent of the clerks at the Préfecture, from which he was to get himself dismissed one of these days—that was in store for him—he would become one of the best. There should be no more of the Café du Gaz, where his office-hours had been spent, his hat once safely on its peg, with a regularity which had begun to attract the attention of his superiors. What he had not been able to do in six years he would do immediately, he would pass the examination for a secretaryship without which he would have to resign himself, at the best, to remaining a mere clerk. No more Bohemianism; he would have a home!

> The firelight and the narrow cone of lamplight;
> musing, with a hand pressed to the brow
> and one's gaze lost in the beloved's eyes;
> the hour of steaming tea, and all books closed;
> the charm of feeling the evening at an end;

delicious tiredness and the adored delay
before the nuptial dawn and the sweet night.
Ah, that! all that, my gentler dream pursues
unfalteringly, across all vain delays,
wildly impatient of the months and weeks!

A wild impatience, that is a faunish warning which must not be overlooked. Though Mathilde is his saviour, his redeemer, she is above all Woman. She is the fruit that till now the famished man has never tasted, that he had believed to be eternally out of his reach; she is the fruit *feminity* in all its freshness and health, with its rich colour and fragrance. All the rooms of this home he built up for himself lead into the nuptial chamber, and here Verlaine is too human for us to accuse him of being too Verlainian. Let us leave aside, then, one or two *"bonnes chansons"* which were a little too ardent, but which, as he tells us, he would not have suppressed, had it not been for his publisher's warning, which had already been responsible for cutting out the tail-piece to the *Fêtes galantes*. In his *Confessions* the poet regrets this and taxes himself with having been puritanical. "Alas, was I not to write other songs," he adds; "for example, *Chansons pour Elle, Odes en son Honneur*, from which, at any rate, the least hypocrisy, or, to be frank, the slightest restraint is, I believe, carefully banished; and I feel no repentance about them; on the contrary, they lull, to rouse them again more ardent, more savage, my desires; all, or almost, for the flesh, now."

These poems, but for the supression of which the volume *La Bonne Chanson* would have been less maidenly, have had less of the Christmas roses about it, are restored to us in the posthumous works. But we must ask Lepelletier to help us to understand the volume as it has reached us in all its diaphanousness:

> He never had a mistress in his youth, in the sense of a prolonged love-affair. . . He did not even visit a woman as a temporary and intermittent lover. He went only to those unfortunate women who sell love like merchandise. He quenched his thirst for love as he did his thirst for absinthe, at the first bar he came across in the street. So he had never been in love. Never did I see Verlaine in his youth give his arm to a woman. He felt himself alone, without a woman friend. . . He never suggested to me that we should make up one of those charming picnics for two, four, six, or even eight, which leave such jolly memories behind.

If Lepelletier, very preoccupied for his part with these charming picnics, never suspected his friend's "first loves" and never saw him, in place of the thrushes which he himself was pursuing, take the blackbirds in revenge, still he enables us to grasp the state of mind the poet was in when, in June 1869, in his twenty-fifth year and after five years of "crooked paths," he met the ideal sweetheart on the high road of "pleasant duty."

Youth, beauty, purity, gaiety, good nature, intelligence, social position—this girl had all these qualities. "She is beautiful and she accepts me." There was a source of wonder never to run dry. When many years later, ruined, debased, and after his discomfiture at Coulommes and his imprisonment at Vouziers he had become "the Beggar in the Sunken Road," he ruminated on the history of this union, and wrote:

Once I saw, I who was thought very ugly, a really
very beautiful woman go by . . .

So she was an angel of freshness and purity, and she
was his! His, the drunkard and the heresiach of love!
His, the slave of Saturn—as he had been, but as he was
no longer now, and never more would be, *never more*,
thanks to Her! After so much materiality, the idealist
that brooded deep down in him aspired to the light and
spread its wings. And is not that the most perfect rose
whose roots plunge farthest into the dung? What is
there astonishing, to anyone who knows a little about
human nature, in the fact that the most delicate poems
that have ever been written on the theme of betrothed
love, such as those beginning:

Before you fade from the sky, pale morning star,

and:

The silver moon gleams in the wood,

should have been sung, not by a Lamartine or a Sully-
Prudhomme, but by a Verlaine!

Youth, beauty . . . she possessed everything, including love. For if the poet was in love he was loved in
return. Lepelletier, who is a careful historian of the
conditions under which the offer of marriage was
accepted (the request was addressed, very curiously, not
to Mathilde or to her parents, but to Charles de Sivry, one
of the suitor's artistic set and a café companion), and he
makes Mathilde's love for Verlaine the primary factor. It
was a case of love at first sight, on both sides, he explains.
Practical considerations—"Verlaine, his looks apart, was
not a match to be despised," certainly entered into it,

both with the parents and with the bride-to-be, but that
was only because love was there already. And among the
elements of which this love was composed I believe we
must number pity. The girl was aware (vaguely, and
without knowing the nature of his "first loves," of
course), of the poet's past behaviour—how could she
not have been, considering her half-brother's friendship
with Verlaine and having already seen him in the literary
salons she visited with her parents, before the famous
meeting in June in de Sivry's rooms? She knew, and
by the contrite sinner's own confession, that she would
not be marrying a model of sobriety on either of the
counts on which the ideal fiancé ought to have been
that. She knew it, and the idea that she would be making
a rescue counted, I am convinced, among the motives
that decided her. This idea minimised in her eyes, dis-
counted, what Lepelletier calls with unnecessary emphasis
the hideousness (ugliness would have done) of her
betrothed.

> "Whilst he was speaking to me," she wrote after-
> wards in her *Mémoires*, "his face seemed to be lit up
> with an interior joy; his expression, which was habi-
> tually hard and dark, became coaxing and tender
> whilst he was looking at me, and his mouth smiling;
> he seemed to be both moved and happy. At that
> moment he ceased to be ugly, and I thought of that
> pretty fairy-story, the Beauty and the Beast, in which
> love transformed the Beast into a Prince Charming."
> (Note 8).

Let us add that this converted sinner, converted by her
and for her sake, was not merely a young man richer
than herself and provided, at least in theory, with a good

job (Note 9). He had the prestige of genius, and was acknowledged the first poet of his generation. In 1869, after the *Poèmes saturniens* and the *Fêtes galantes*, Verlaine already held the position, or at least it rested with him to do so or not, of leader of a school. Mathilde, who lived in a set keenly interested in literature and art, had been bitten herself by the writing-bug. At sixteen she wrote verses as badly as anyone could, but not without energy; she tried to mimic Banville and Baudelaire, and on top of that she used to sketch. Lepelletier does not tell us this, but I discovered it from Mathilde's note-books and albums (Note 10). It was merely a child's amusement, and there was no need for her husband to be perturbed, she was not of the stuff blue-stockings are made of. After her divorce and re-marriage, Mathilde Mauté made a perfect wife and mother.

II.   THE ENGAGEMENT AND THE HONEYMOON

Unfortunately, the poet-lover—and the beloved—may propose, but Drink disposes (Note 11). Verlaine was to drink less during the period of their engagement, but as for thinking that he became temperate again, that is quite another matter; and if Mathilde assures us that he did, in her *Mémoires*, that is because she did not accompany him to the Cafés Gaz, Delta, Madrid and all the rest. Lepelletier expresses serious doubts, not, certainly, as to the poet's sincere intention of abstaining from the *accursed liquors*, but as to his complete success. And you will not think this malevolence on his part, if you turn to a note contained in their *Correspondance* which is dated 1870, and was certainly written before the

marriage, which took place on August 11th, when war
had broken out and Lepelletier was mobilised.

> "Abominable drunkard," exclaims the poet to his
> friend, reminding him that he had to lunch with
> the future parents-in-law that day in the rue Nicolet,
> "I am waiting for you. Don't make any allusion to
> my being canned yesterday. I think I have managed,
> by some miracle of hypocrisy, to conceal how lit up
> I was after all yesterday's absinthes, bitters and
> bocks."

A short note, but it is a significant warning as to what
was awaiting the Verlaine household!
Mathilde writes:

> During the fourteen months of our engagement and
> the first year of our marriage Verlaine was kind,
> tender, affectionate and gay; yes, gay with a good-
> natured, sane and sociable gaiety. He so completely
> ceased drinking that those who had known him
> before his marriage thought him cured for ever,
> and my parents and I never suspected that he had
> been a drunkard. We only learnt it too late, alas!

Those "fourteen months of our engagement" must be
reduced by at least a quarter, as regards the possibility
of Mathilde's observing her future husband's sobriety—
and he knew how to conceal his intoxicated states with
such skill! For in the summer of 1869 they were separated during June and a part of July, whilst Verlaine
was staying at Fampoux; then Mathilde went for a holiday to Normandy, from which she did not return till
September; *La Bonne Chanson* is largely made up of poems

sent to her during this separation. In the spring of 1870
they had again to be parted, as the girl was suffering
from small-pox. This creature of impulse who, immediately after the interview in June at which he had fallen
in love, without warning a soul or even taking the trouble—*proh pudor bureaucratica!*—to ask for leave, left
Paris in a state of febrile excitement to which, no doubt,
alcoholism contributed as much as love—this impulsive
creature was compelled, before his marriage, to live
through a period ill-suited to the calming of his "wild
impatience with the months and weeks." A succession
of events laid down step by step, one might say, "by
the logic of a malign Influence," conspired against this
subject of Saturn. In those last months of the Second
Empire Verlaine had become a declared Republican
(Note 12), a fervent supporter of a militant policy, at
least of the sort that legislates from the benches of esta-
minets, and was already qualifying himself for the post
of Chief of the Press Bureau with which the Commune
invested him. A fortnight before the date fixed for his
marriage his enervation was so pronounced that he was
advised to go into the country. On his return three days
before the ceremony he was the spectator—his *Confessions* relate this saturnine episode in detail—when a
friend of his blew out his brains, after having warned
him that he was going to do it and entrusted him with
seeing to his funeral arrangements. On his return from
the cemetery, the day before his marriage, he dropped in
at the Café de Madrid, which was crowded with Opposition journalists excited by the news of one of the early
French defeats, at first announced as a great victory. He
was the most worked-up of all, and his shouts of *Vive
la République* reached such a pitch that he would have

been dragged off by the police but for the exertions of his friends. And then, after several libations in honour of his deliverance, he regained Batignolles only to come on a decree calling to the Colours the unmarried men of the 1844-5 class:

> For the moment his patriotic emotions evaporated; he no longer dreamt of shouting *Vive la République*, nor long live anything else. Giving the table a terrible blow with his fist, he cried out, "My marriage is . . . done for." And with that he ordered another absinthe and drank it with a wild expression.

As for their year of happiness, the "husband from the slums" did not wait twelve months before revealing himself—far from it. His service in the National Guard, in the sector of the southern forts, between Issy and Montrouge, was not spent with only his old-fashioned rifle in his fist; and this is the moment at which, according to his *Confessions*, he first raised his hand against his wife.

> National defence, Lepelletier banters at this point, made the citizen-soldiers very thirsty. Verlaine promptly became the equal of the heavy drinkers of the battalion, in which coopers and wine-sellers' men, all workmen or inhabitants of Bercy employed in the liquor-trade, were in the majority. It was not long before he returned to the conjugal home in a state of jollity. He vexed his wife and made her anxious. Perhaps one evening he became too expansively jingoistic or uxorious; the young wife then left their home for the first time and fled for refuge

to her parents in Montmartre. The marriage was
hardly six months old. . .

and the ink had not yet dried on the enthusiastic pages of
La Bonne Chanson.

Neither the hardships of the Siege nor the coming
of the Commune tended to de-saturnise the author of the
Poèmes saturniens. In March, Verlaine, instead of rejoin-
ing the public services at Versailles as the Government
had ordered, or better—what an opportunity for such a
Civil Servant—staying at home, actively collaborated
with the insurgents. Quite unconsciously, rather against
his will—according to Lepelletier—from the sheer
affection of the bureaucrat for his leather-topped stool,
he allowed himself to be nominated to the position of
Chief of the Press Bureau! Lepelletier is making fun of
us, and really the poet's fidelity to his office can scarcely
be called as evidence. No; at that moment Verlaine acted
with all the impulsiveness characteristic of him, as he had
done just before at the Café de Madrid, as he would do
later when, on his first journey to London with Rimbaud,
he mingled with the Communist refugees and wrote in
the political sheets Vermersch edited; as he would do
later still, when he wrote *Sagesse,* and that *Voyage en
France par un Français,* in which he is a more ardent
champion of the throne and altar, and a stauncher churchman than Veuillot himself. Whatever one's opinion of
either of the two political creeds he espoused, why deny
that he embraced the first with as much fervour as the
second? Why not realise that if he went to the extreme
limit of Catholic toryism until the time when

Woman had quite dominated him again,

it was because he had first gone to the extreme limit of anti-religious anarchism. The violent insults directed against the Prince Imperial which are scattered through his *Croquis Londoniens* of 1872 ensure for us the palinode inspired by the Prince's death in 1879:

> Prince, who hast died a soldier's death for France,
> Soul surely saved,
> Brave, spotless youth, cut off full of promise,
> I love and salute you.
> In my early years, brought up in violent doctrines,
> I detested your young life. . .
> I admire your fate and all in tears adore.

It was to explain such characters as his that the proverb "extremes meet" was invented. On the 18th March, 1871, and the following days there was not a more excited antagonist of Versailles than this poet; and the terrible Raoul Rigault, Procureur of the Commune, to whom he was attached by a friendship of long standing, made no mistake in granting him a post the importance of which cannot be denied. Verlaine, then, threw himself into it with all his heart, but that, with him, does not mean that he made much headway. I should not be surprised if the greater part of his activity turned out to consist of lengthy palavers accompanied by much smoking and drinking; nor if he should have been not the last rat to leave the sinking ship. But with the foundering of the Commune these potations had to cease, for terror counselled the late Chief of the Press Bureau, now hidden in his parents-in-law's house in the rue Nicolet, against frequenting the cafés. But as his fears became increasingly sharp and he believed that he was about to be denounced to the authorities, Verlaine went away to Fampoux, taking with him Mathilde, who had been pregnant for five months. He went away full of horror for the "accursed liquors"; he was to return at the end of September, reassured of his fears and ready for that domestic existence which he led till his flight from his home, in the following July, with Rimbaud.

III. DOMESTICITY

September 1871 to July 1872: that is the period during which Verlaine was sinking into, and was finally swallowed up by, the most noisome swamp of Bohemianism into which a great poet has ever fallen. And the stages of this process are recorded in a document which shall be allowed to speak for itself.

This document is the application that in September 1872 Mathilde Mauté presented to the Tribunal de la Seine in support of her petition for a judicial separation; or, rather, that part of the application which enumerates the facts she desires to be allowed to prove, both by documents and witnesses, in the ordinary legal way (Note 13). It is headed by a preamble in which it is recalled that the marriage took place on August 11th, 1870, and that a boy was born of it on October 30th, 1871. The marriage "was instituted under the most favourable auspices; indeed, it appeared during the first year to be completely satisfactory, both to the couple and to their relatives." Unfortunately, for about a year past "Verlaine has altered his behaviour, associating with bad companions and giving way to drink and to absinthe," abuses which "have thrown him into a state of over-excitation resembling delirium tremens." As an effect of this there occurred "scenes of the gravest kind, endangering the lives of his wife and his child." Besides this, "the acquaintance he had made with an Arthur Rimbaud, a young man of eighteen, had exercised a most pernicious influence on him," revealing to the petitioner, "evidence of the most monstrous immorality."

The preamble goes on to inform us that in February 1872 Madame Verlaine, to escape from her husband's violences, had begun a suit against him for a simple separation, but that on promises from him she had consented to drop it. That, "not only had she soon become the object of fresh brutalities," but that "her efforts to tear her husband away from the ruinous domination of Rimbaud had been in vain." After that the declaration unrolls its eleven sections

Like a long serpent that unrolls its coils,

but which, unhappily for the defendant, the sword of Justice was not cut in pieces.

1. In the month of September 1871, the husband and wife came to live with the young woman's parents, the petitioner hoping that her parents' presence would compel her husband to exercise some restraint in his conduct and to show some consideration for her; and also so that she might lie-in under the most favourable conditions; for from this period Verlaine gave way to absinthe-drinking and was associated with Rimbaud, who already had the greatest influence over him.

2. On November 15th, 1871, just fifteen days after his wife had given birth, Verlaine, having been

present at the first performance of Coppée's *l'Aban-donnée*, stayed to supper with his friends and passed a part of the night in drinking; when he returned home he was in an indescribable state of intoxication, and without any pretext and with no regard for the health of his wife and the child she was nursing, created a most violent scene, which only ceased on the arrival of M. Mauté, who rushed to his daughter's protection. Verlaine had to be persuaded to go for a walk to calm his excitation.

3. From this time onward Verlaine went more and more to the café, often passing whole days there and a part of the night, drinking alcoholic liquors and absinthe principally. He returned at all hours of the night in a besotted condition, forcing quarrels on his wife, and, moreover, to the very legitimate observations she made on his conduct and the ruinous consequences it might have for his health and his financial position, he replied only with violences and continued his slothful and brutalising way of life.

4. On January 13th, 1872, Madame Verlaine being indisposed, had been obliged to stay in bed and had not been able to go down to dinner; her husband, as often happened, did not arrive till the end of the meal, and when that was over he went up to his wife and without even enquiring about her health, tried to pick a quarrel with her about a cup of coffee he had just had and declared he would go to the café to get another; then, as Madame Verlaine did not answer, he said: "Your calm, your composure, exasperates me; I have had enough of it." Then, rising to a paroxysm of fury, he roughly seized his child and flung him violently on to the bed, at the

risk of killing him; then, grasping his wife by the wrists, which he tore with his nails, he thrust her on to the bed, knelt on her and violently pressed her throat to strangle her. Hearing the plaintiff's screams, M. and Mme Mauté rushed into the room and had great difficulty in making him release his hold and getting him out of the room.

5. The next day Verlaine, who had promised to be more composed in future, not to make scenes with his wife and to give some apology to his parents-in-law neglected to, and even refused to, embrace his wife, saying: "That sort of thing is stupid; it's not worth the bother." The same evening he did not come in to dinner nor return till midnight. The petitioner was in bed and scarcely recovered from the agitation of the previous evening, so that her father begged M. Verlaine not to awaken his young wife; but he paid no attention to these remarks, and forced his wife to come and open the door to him, and was only persuaded to withdraw on the repeated admonishments of M. Mauté. He then went down the stairs, declaring that he was not going out, but was going away for ever, never to come back to his wife.

6. Since then, in fact, Verlaine had never returned to his wife in the rue Nicolet. He had gone to stay with his mother, though not in fact always living with her; and he did not alter his habits of going to the café and drinking in any way; he did not cease threatening to kill his wife and her parents; in short, his delirium tremens had reached such a pitch that, to escape the danger menacing herself and her child, Madame Verlaine decided to draw up her petition

G

for a separation, and whilst awaiting the hearing before M. le Président she went to the south of France for a time with her father, in order to recuperate from the serious moral and physical strain she had been subjected to. After several postponements, due to the benevolence of M. le Président, she yielded to the solicitations and promises of her husband and consented to go back to him and not to pursue her petition; but the scenes of violence recommenced immediately and he continued to get drunk several times a week.

7. On May 9th, 1872, Ascension Day, Verlaine returned at night completely under the influence of wine, and he was hardly in bed when he reproached his wife most violently because her father had returned; then, working himself up without any motive, he began to hit his wife and maltreat her with the utmost brutality, and as she said to him, "You are a coward, you would do better to kill me," he took a match, struck it and brought it close to his wife's hair to set it alight. The next day everyone could see the marks of Verlaine's violence; his wife had a broken lip and a lump on her forehead.

8. About the middle of June the couple went to dinner with the widow Verlaine; there, without any sort of motive, Verlaine upbraided his wife and, drawing a knife from his pocket, threatened to kill her. After an hour's struggle she succeeded in running for safety to the house of one of their friends, who secretly took her back to her father. A very short time afterwards Verlaine arrived there, and as Madame Mauté wanted to stop him going into the room where his wife had taken refuge,

he was about to ill-use her, when M. Mauté himself
came to her assistance; he was met with blows from a
loaded cane, and it was only by knocking Verlaine
down and taking his cane from him that he put an
end to his violence and forced him to calm himself.
9. On July 7th Verlaine did not return home,
where he had left his wife ill and waiting for the
doctor he had promised to go and fetch. After
three days of enquiries amongst all her husband's
friends, and even at the Morgue, the petitioner
learnt that he had left for Brussels at two o'clock
that day with Rimbaud, thus abandoning his wife
and child; and soon afterwards he wrote for his
belongings to be sent to him.
10. The petitioner, with the last degree of devotion
and self-abnegation, herself journeyed to Brussels,
accompanied by her mother, on July 21st, in the
hope of bringing him back and of afterwards being
able to assist him to escape from the ruinous temptations that beset him. There the gravest admissions
were made to her by her husband himself, but as the
young woman, not completely understanding,
mistook the meaning of his words, she succeeded
in getting him to promise to return, and they left
together for Paris. But at Quievrain, where all the
passengers were obliged to leave the train for the
Customs examination, Verlaine refused to get into
the train again, and left his wife to go on alone with
her mother.
11. On their return to Paris she received the most
monstrous revelations as to her husband's conduct,
and his letters left her no more doubt as to the nature
of his relations with Rimbaud.

Of the letters which the Tribunal had in front of them before declaring in a judgment given April 24th, 1874, that the defendant's correspondence "establishes that he had immoral relations with a young man," we know the contents of the one sent from Quievrain.

"Verlaine refused to get into the train again," the declaration says. Mathilde, in her *Mémoires*, describes how she and her mother, after having searched for him and called to him all over the station, observed him on the platform just as the porters were shutting the carriage doors. "Jump in quickly," my mother called out to him.

"No, I am staying," he answered, cramming his hat down on his head with a blow of his fist.

She was never to see him again, but when back in Paris she received this love letter from him, an exhibit whose absence from among the documentary evidence in this Bohemian marriage would have been regrettable:

You wretched red-headed elf, Princess Sneak,* you bug, a nip of the fingers, and into the chamber with you; you have ruined everything; you have perhaps broken my friend's heart. I am going back to Rimbaud, if he will have anything more to do with me after this betrayal you have made me commit. (Note 14).

*Textually, *Princesse Souris*, but *souris* (mouse) is the term for a woman who goes through her husband's pockets whilst he is asleep, and judging from the references to his wife in Verlaine's letters, I think that is the particular insult he intended.

"COMPANIONS IN HELL"

1. WITH RIMBAUD

Immediately Verlaine had sent this letter, which had been inspired by absinthe, he lost all memory of it; for, had he not done so, he would not still have dared, for all his self-assurance, to cite "my interview with my wife at Brussels" as a noteworthy example of the shameful way Mathilde and her parents behaved towards him— "I who am all tenderness and artlessness, alas!"

That letter is an example of those demented actions due to alcohol which in his *Confessions* he terms merely follies: "I shall later have to relate many, many other follies due to the abuse of that terrible thing—drink; and among drinks that abuse itself, source of madness and crime, idiocy and shame—absinthe." He leaves off these reminiscences, which are so alive and begin so promisingly, at the moment of Rimbaud's arrival on the scene, but Madame Verlaine's petition fills in the gap as regards the story of their married life from September 1871. We have already disclosed this in order to defend the poet's wife against the stupid reproaches of the official and certainly invaluable biographer, Lepelletier, who in this affair draws quite the wrong moral. He is the amplifier of such lines as:

You have not been wholly patient . . .
Being, thanks to you, the least happy of men .
Yet here am I, filled with chaste forgiveness

103

of which *Birds in the Night* is so harmoniously composed. What Lepelletier gives us, as a lawyer uniquely occupied with his client's interests, is the system of defence which, in London on the eve of the hearing of the case, Pauvre Lélian's subconsciousness and cunning elaborated with the help of drink. This defence is buttressed by many passages in his work, but the *Confessions* (for which we should praise them) do not attempt to maintain it; yet it has been accepted by everybody, until our disclosures. Now that this injustice has been corrected the petition must be produced, not as hostile evidence, but in the poet's interests, as a demonstration of his mental irresponsibility. It was alcohol working in him, not he himself.

During the second year of his marriage he was living, as the petition says, in a state of excitation bordering on delirium tremens. And he lived in the same state from July 7th, 1872, the day of his departure with Rimbaud, till July 12th, 1873, the day of the revolver shots in Brussels. But the concubinage of the Foolish Virgin and the Satanic Bridegroom* was by no means delayed till the flight into Belgium; it dates from the end of September 1871; that is to say, from the day when "the Child of mysterious delicacies" got off the train from Charleville. Already in the grip of the "accursed liquors" once more, the erotomaniac, whose wife was not available (she bore her child on October 30th), returned to his "first loves." And the attitude of the two friends, sometimes flaunted barefacedly as is proved by a poem in *Hombres:*

*Characters in Rimbaud's *Une Saison en Enfer* representing Verlaine and himself respectively, in the section which allegorically describes their relationship. (T)

> In this café crammed with imbeciles we two
> alone represented the so-called hideous vice of
> being "for men" . . .

became so pronounced by the following July that it
must be considered one of the reasons—the principal
one perhaps—for their going away. The history of the
relations of Rimbaud and Verlaine, then, falls into two
periods.

The first is Parisian. It runs parallel to Verlaine's
married life and is broken by quarrels which coincide
with the different reconciliations of husband and wife;
the result of one of which was Rimbaud's return to his
home in the Ardennes and Mathilde's abandonment of
her first petition for a separation.

The second is Anglo-Belgian, in the course of which
the Damned Couple were to separate and come together
again, Rimbaud crossing the Channel three times. This
second period was, no less than the first, passed under
the guidance of alcohol; and the cry that Verlaine was to
utter, licking his lips, in his bragging poem *Laeti et
Errabundi:*

> Among other blameworthy excesses, I believe that
> we drank of everything, from the greatest wines of
> France down to beer and stout, not to mention
> spirits that are supposed to be formidable . . .

applies as truly to Brussels and London as to Paris. In
this respect the Season in Hell that the author of *La
Bonne Chanson* must have made Mathilde spend is the
perfect equivalent of that which he and Rimbaud were to
lead together. This is revealed by Verlaine's letters as
well as by many passages in the works of each of them,

and also by the documents relating to the Brussels assault.

Thus, whether we observe Verlaine when he is about to sever the roots that attach him to a regular existence, or thrusting into a life of the worst irregularity roots that it will never be possible to sever, he provides us with a moral. He disengages what is the principal element that goes to the making of what may be called *integral*, or as it ought to be called after him, *Saturnian* Bohemianism. He shows that the essential of this Bohemian life, whether sedentary or wandering, solitary or with a companion-in-hell, is intemperance; just as the essential of the bourgeois life (integral or not . . . at any rate that within the limits of which most great poets have lived) is sobriety.

To say "bourgeois life" is to say "home"; and it is lack of a home even more than lack of money that is characteristic of Bohemianism. So, really to see into Verlaine and into his work, we must appreciate the force and constancy of the instinct which unceasingly turns back his thoughts towards the picture of a home. For, to soothe himself in his London loneliness in the moments of half-lucidity snatched from drunkenness, he dreams of making a new nest—he who had just applied so much energy to the destruction of the old one, so cosy, and equipped with all the advantages his desires had so ardently imagined:

> I am about to change my way of life here. Rimbaud is going back to Charleville this week and my mother is coming here. Her presence, apart from the immense pleasure it will be to me, will be very useful from the point of view of *respectability*.

Respectability! Verlaine thirsted for it all his life. Less than for love, alcohol and poetry, that goes without saying, but ardently none the less; and right up to the end of his life we shall find him announcing as imminent: "if my ill-luck ceases to pursue me, the extreme worthiness of my life," and promising to show us "the man I can be—meticulous, dignified and everything! . . ." But at this time, at the end of 1872, he caressed the idea of living with his mother "in a little house in one of the cheaper parts of London," where "life is a hundred times less expensive than in Paris, the climate a hundred times healthier, and work infinitely easier to find." In those circumstances his life "would become completely happy again, and having quite forgotten those vile people" who were persecuting him (his wife and parents-in-law), he would re-create the tranquility he needed and —who knows?—perhaps marry again. Heavens! he "deserved that compensation":

> I do not see why, after having suffered and implored so much, and having forgiven so much when I was being monstrously attacked, when my saintly mother was insulted and wounded in all her affections, after all this ingratitude, I do not see why I should renounce my hope of the joys of an honest union.

It is not only the Mayor of Montmartre who can marry people; there are civilian officials in England, too. No doubt, he says, Lepelletier will think him "sunk deep in Anglophilia" after "having begun by vomiting so many complaints (in part legitimate)" against the Island and its inhabitants. But the inhabitants, both men and women, are not so much to be despised after all.

English life, when seen more closely, has its points. And, then, "family life, which is stupid in France because it has no power, is so thoroughly organised here that even the most Bohemian let themselves be caught."

Do not laugh at this obsession. With the assistance of religion, we owe to it such songs in praise of family happiness and an orderly existence, as:

> The little home, the little nest . . .

or

> Oh, God, My God, life there is calm and
> simple. . .

But Pauvre Lélian's congenital antipathy for Bohemianism once showed itself amusingly in an episode which is worth relating.

It took place in December, 1893. The poet had returned from England, where he had been giving some lectures, and his purse was well stuffed:

> He had at times a little money
> And feasted his companions.
> Lucullus?—No, Trimalchio,

as he explains in *Parallèlement*. On the evening of his return he took a fancy to playing the Trimalchio by taking two friends who had dined at his expense to supper in Montmartre. On the way there the trio swelled to a dozen. They drank, ate, talked, recited and sang, Verlaine encouraging the company . . . and the proprietor of the bar by taking out his wallet every time the waiter was called for an order. But when the bill arrived, seeing the amount it was and finding that he was the only person there who had any money, he flew into a rage. He seized the stick with which he used to drag his bad leg along and, holding it at arm's length, wildly traced a magic semicircle in front of him, shouting: "No Bohemians here!"

Everybody leapt out of the way except a certain Brandenburger, the poorest devil in the party and the worst intruder, who had eaten and drunk so well that he was snoring in his chair. The blow caught him on the neck and flung him on the floor among the plates and glasses not less inanimate than they. As a result he was unconscious such a long time that Pauvre Lélian— ought we to call him poor or rich on this occasion?— settled the bill without further resistance.

This Brandenburger, an obscure contributor to Jules Roques's *Courrier français*, was famous in the Montmartre laundries of the day. He possessed two shirts in all. When one was dirty he used to take it off in his laundress's shop and put on the clean one there. But let us leave farce and return to the serious drama.

II.   THE BRUSSELS SHOOTING

The attempt at murder of which Rimbaud was the victim was an alcoholic crime, if there ever was one. The actual damage done was slight—a bullet in the wrist easily extracted after a few days in hospital, leaving a wound which healed quickly and had no after effects, but the crime is a perfect example of an attempted murder and one which, to use the words of the Penal Code, "only failed in its intention through circumstances independent of the perpetrator's will." According to the

letter of the law it would even have been murder in the
first degree, for there was no disputing its premeditation;
there was the purchase of the revolver a few hours
before the drama; then the fact that Verlaine showed it
to Rimbaud with the words: "It's for you; for me; for
everybody," and his taking care to shut and lock the
door which led to the landing. For several reasons,
certainly to be approved, the Public Prosecutor in
Brussels treated this dreadful crime as a simple case of
assault and wounding; but Lepelletier is really absurd
when he treats the affair as if the offence had been a
laughing matter which ought not to have had any legal
consequences at all; and when he reproaches the judges
for a harshness which can only be explained, according
to him, by the damaging information they had received
about Verlaine's political past.

But whatever name one gives it and whatever way one
judges it, Verlaine's action was the logical culmination
of the two years of intoxication the unfortunate man
had gone through. I do not intend to describe the circumstances which gradually led up to it; I have done so
elsewhere, and it is a long and complicated story impossible to condense. In all probability, however, Rimbaud saved Mathilde. To not a few moments of the
period that elapsed between Arthur's first departure
from London, at the end of 1872, and the shooting,
might this refrain of a ballade in *Parallèlement* be applied :

But for my part, I see red. . .

As early as in one of his first letters to Lepelletier from
London, 24th September, 1872, the poet speaks of being
"the *provoked* instrument of *divine* Justice," since human
justice remained at the disposition of his wicked mate

and her abominable parents. But loneliness was the least supportable of all evils to our Saturnian subject, and when he saw himself deprived both of his friend and his wife, drink drove him finally demented. Till as late as July 1873 he retained the hope—it shows how mad he was—that Mathilde would let herself be caught again; and the hope, scarcely less mad, that he could hold Rimbaud. On July 12th these two hopes were both ruined. At Brussels his good mother, whom he had sent on an embassy to the rue Nicolet, reported the failure of her mission; at Brussels, Arthur, whom he had just abandoned in London because he counted on hearing in Brussels that his wife would come back to him, Arthur informed him that their reconciliation of May (after he had gone back once again to his Ardennes) had been, without appeal, their last. To go to Paris in order to "execute justice on his wife and parents-in-law" (his words as reported by Rimbaud in his evidence), that was easier to talk about than to do. For had he not last year in London, he, the ex-Chief of the Communist Press Bureau, who had been miraculously overlooked by the counter-revolution, been so imprudent as to contribute to the anti-Governmental paper Vermersch edited!* And as a consequence of that, he had had something to tell Lepelletier when he wrote to him in the middle of April, from Jehonville, where he had gone to be near Rimbaud and take him back to London:

> I do not know if you have learnt of my leaving London, but, at any rate, I can tell you that my absence from the great city is only temporary, for

---

*L'Avenir, a short-lived periodical issued in Soho by the refugees from the Commune, which naturally attacked a policy which was actively pursuing the few surviving Communists. (T)

I have proved only too well that Paris and France will be dangerous for me a long while yet.

This unfortunate fact was proved by my attempt to travel by Newhaven and Dieppe, and I only owe it to a providential chance, if I dare call it so, and to a conversation in execrable English overheard *on the boat* an hour before it sailed (the said conversation being between some men in military overcoats, with white moustaches), that I am not ʹat this moment within *la belle France*, groaning on the straw in the cells, not less damp than preventive, of this Republic of ours.

A real hallucination, or imaginary? Verlaine is quite capable of having invented it to excite Lepelletier's pity, but the sense of fear it indicates is very real.

So, on July 12th, with the revolver loaded in his pocket, after having specially devoted forty-eight hours (Rimbaud having arrived from London on the morning of the 10th) to giving a final polish with liqueurs to the layer of alcoholism that had been forming for so many months, what was Verlaine to do? He is the very innocent victim, "I who am all tenderness and artlessness, alas!" of his wife's folly and spite; he is less innocently, he admits, the victim of his friend, but his victim none the less. For was it not to follow that friend, in July last year, that he "abandonned all his human obligations"? The more guilty of the two is not within reach of his avenging arm, but he has a hold on the other one. He sees Rimbaud definitely refusing, in spite of so many tears and supplications, to accompany him to London (where, he has forgotten already, he had abandoned him without any consideration a few days before) or to

Paris either. He will deal Rimbaud his deserts as soon as drink has worked him up to the necessary pitch.

The majority of crimes of passion are acts of justice visualised in this way. The assailant, whether stimulated by alcohol or not, but with all the greater force if he is, is one who, primarily, is passionately obsessed with himself—a boundless egoist. He is incapable of being distressed by the thought of the harm he is doing another person; often incapable even of recognising that he is harming a person, as Verlaine was with regard to Mathilde; but his own skin is so sensitive that he can call the mere efforts his victim makes to escape him attacks on himself; odious attacks. And as regards Rimbaud, at that actual moment the righteousness of the grievances he was nursing against him burst on Verlaine's demented mind with as much force as the shots he was about to fire.

III.   THE MONS TREATMENT

But, since the act was destined, we may be thankful that it occurred under these circumstances and with these consequences, and consider them fortunate. In the first place because, as regards the victim, these consequences were unimportant and because we cannot be sure that the revolver would have been so harmless had it been fired in the rue Nicolet. And, further, because the victim was not wholly innocent, whilst had it not been for him an innocent person, and one already to be pitied, ran the risk of being hit, and in the rue Nicolet there might even have been a number of victims. And the last and strongest reason why we may consider them fortunate—I say strongest, because here we are no

longer dealing in hypotheses—is because, had it not
been for this assault in Brussels, Verlaine would have
been lost to poetry.

If he had not seen red in July, 1873, if he had been,
like so many others in the grip of alcohol, a harmless
imbecile, it would not have been long before he had
been the inmate of a padded cell. The gaol was preferable.
On July 12th he was still capable, not of being completely, but of being temporarily cured, and so given the
time to write *Sagesse, Jadis et Naguère*, and *Parallèlement*—
not to speak of his later productions, which could have
been dispensed with. And could he have undergone this
treatment anywhere except where the Brussels Courts
sent him? To believe so one would have to be very
ignorant of the course his life ran.

To write *Sagesse*, Verlaine had first of all to be put into
a state of remorse, of repentance. And he could only
experience such a state after a catastrophe of this kind.
And afterwards he had to be retained, maintained, in this
state for a considerable period. Where could this have
been done except in the place where he was kept from
July 1873 till January 1875?

Sagesse is an act of contrition, a cry of hope, just as *La
Bonne Chanson* had been. The ill-starred Bohemian here
invokes God and the Virgin Mary with the same impulsiveness as he had recently invoked the Beloved, and
Woman:

> My God said to me: My son, you must love me. . .
> You must love me. I am the universal kiss. . .
> I desire to love none now but my mother Mary. . .

the erotomaniac diverts into the channel of divine love
the torrent of sensibility which before had been devoted

to profane love, and as sincerely, as ardently, and even
more eloquently than ever. The vision of the Paradise
won is substituted for that of the Home he has lost. In
this way Verlaine tasted joys at Mons to which, I have
no doubt, he would have preferred those of freedom,
but which were none the less real for being compulsory.
When he recalled them later it was to evoke with pleasure,
even in its physical details, the memory of his prison:

Once upon a time I dwelt in the best of mansions. . .

Can one believe that without this eighteen months
imprisonment he would have been capable of regaining
the full possession of his genius? Notice that between
his *La Bonne Chanson*, composed during the winter of 1869
and the spring of 1870, and the revolver-shot at Brussels—that is, in three years and a half—he produced
nothing but his *Romances sans Paroles*, hardly four hundred and fifty lines of verse. Yet Verlaine was born gifted
with a fecundity on the same scale as that of the great
poets, and he never lost his taste for making verses.
We must conclude that alcohol killed his poetic faculty
as it has done that of so many others—that of Musset, for
example, of Baudelaire, and of Rimbaud. For "drink" is
as injurious to the poet as to the philistine; I mean exces-
sive drinking, for it is possible that to certain tempera-
ments, and taken in moderate quantities, it may act as a
spiritual aperitif. But, it will be asked, what about Raoul
Ponchon? Ponchon is a single example against twenty
that the history of poetry can show to the contrary; and
then Ponchon's method of drinking had no relation to
Verlaine's. The one drank like a philosopher, the other
like a madman.

What has been said of *Sagesse* may be applied to

Parallèlement also, for a large number of the poems in that volume were written or conceived in Mons prison; as we know, this collection was to have been called *Cellulairement*. The new title is more suitable, for the latter adverb is as appropriate to Verlaine's sacred volume as to his human . . . all too human, volume! During his eighteen months in Mons, Verlaine wrote or sketched out, too, more than one of the poems which were to make up other volumes besides the two named above. And it must be pointed out, to show that the addiction to alcohol was poetic suicide for him, that of the two volumes which were yet to be of importance in his work, *Jadis et Naguère* and *Amour*, the greater part of the first consists of poems written before he was thirty, as was partly the case with *Parallèlement*, too (Note 15).

Thus the treatment at Mons delayed the sterility of this poet who was built for a long and abundant productive life, had he not drunk. It procured his Muse a respite from suicide of extreme importance; besides the probability that without it (or without an analagous regimen that Verlaine, if there had been no Brussels drama, might have managed to follow elsewhere) he would not have developed into a Catholic poet, and certainly not into a poet of the prison; so that in that respect French poetry would still have had only Villon. But before the Brussels affair Verlaine's Muse had received the wound from which she was only to recover for a while. And Literature gained nothing, if not from the vices with which Pauvre Lélian was afflicted (except so far as those vices conditioned his poetry, for those vices formed him into the poet we should otherwise have lacked, the poet of remorse and repentance), at least it gained nothing from the pitiable destiny his succumbing to these vices ensured him.

Desinit in piscem . . . there is no other great poet to whom the image applies so well. If we add, as perhaps we ought, to the eight important volumes Verlaine has left us (from the *Poèmes saturniens* to *Amour*) a third of the contents of *Bonheur*, then it would be that third the production of which is closer in date to the publication of *Amour* than of *Bonheur* itself. Thus amputated of its later portion, *Chansons pour Elle*, *Liturgies intimes*, *Odes en son Honneur*, *Chair*, etc. Verlaine's work is seen to be as unimpressive in amount as it is precious in quality. And among these qualities must be numbered two which render poets legitimately fertile: variety in the thought and virtuosity in technique. I do not regret the fact that a poet of Baudelaire's genius should have left us only some four thousand lines, for it seems to me that in *Les Fleurs du Mal* we have Baudelaire wholly and completely. But I never meditate on those eight earlier volumes without regretting that Pauvre Lélian, instead of being restricted to less than eight thousand lines— that count—should not have doubled or trebled that amount.

COUNTRY LIFE

V. COUNTRY LIFE

I. THE ITINERANT SCHOOLMASTER

During the twenty-one years left him to live after his release from the Mons prison, that is, from January 16th, 1875, till January 8th, 1896, Verlaine's Bohemianism falls into three clearly-defined sections, which may be named the school-teaching, the farming and the Parisian periods.

The first, which ended in the year 1879, hardly deserves to be called Bohemian, certainly not Saturnian. The poet succeeded in establishing himself on the plane of respectability, and but for the influence of his planet Saturn would have remained there finally. For his effort was fervid and vigorous, though it all but turned out very badly at the start.

The ex-prisoner at first went to stay with his mother at the house of some relatives at Fampoux. There he decided to earn his living in the only profession that answered both to his tastes and his qualifications. He would go and teach French in England. But, and this is the deplorable outset, he wanted to go to England with Rimbaud.

He accepted with the resignation counselled by religion the decree of separation that had been pronounced on the previous 24th April. He accepted it also *parallèlement*,* for since the friend had bewitched him he

*A mundane motive balanced the religious one, as the mundane themes of the poems in *Parallèlement* balanced the sacred ones of *Sagesse*. (T)

had cared little about the wife, and at this moment he was as subjugated as ever to the spell.

If we do not let ourselves be caught in the trap of his poems and letters we shall see that Verlaine had felt very little attachment to Mathilde at the time of Rimbaud's coming on the scene, and that once Rimbaud was there, he had detached himself from her completely. And if the indignation in his references to the suit she was bringing against him was sincere (the product of his spoilt-child egoism and his alcoholic dementia), his supplications were less so. They were dictated much more by his fear of the consequences the case would have for him, as defendant, than by any love he had for the petitioner. No doubt he often turned towards his wife again; as often as, but not more often than, he quarrelled with his friend. If he longed for Mathilde it was with desire, not with love, even in the least idealistic or altruistic sense of the word—some of his letters to Lepelletier which are accompanied with drawings leave us in no doubt as to the ithyphallic nature of his desires. And under the influence of loneliness, which was insupportable to a temperament so excessively sociable as his, remorse and repentance might deceive him as to his own feelings. Then he was to write the fairest flower that the anthology of contrition can show; *London Bridge*, a poem which the psychologist who works for the good of poetry ought continually to draw attention to, for two reasons. In the first place, because this great poet produced nothing more beautiful; secondly, because, as it was unknown till quite recently, it is not given in his collected works:

Watch these dark waters, this broad, miry stream, that sweeps down all the city's filthy rubbish, and

you will see a gleam of light shine for an instant,
a spangle of gold where the sun plays.

And if you can look into my heart now, perhaps
you will see a faint radiance there. It is just a
memory of her first beauty, and it is enough, you
see, to assuage it.

For hope is like the shining sun; they have both
the power to create this radiance. Some divine
dreams for a broken heart and such gleams of gold
on a miry stream.

This confession was written at the same time as the
Romances sans paroles, and in a good edition of Verlaine
it would be replaced amongst them. It would balance
Birds in the Night; it is as sincere, as spontaneous as that
other confession, for all its divine harmony, is calculated:
an amalgam of cunning and unconsciousness, of that
kind of cunning which moral unconsciousness does not
merely not inhibit, but actually provokes.

So, whilst the poet was to make *Birds in the Night* the
centre, the keystone of his Machiavellian *Romances sans
paroles,* he excluded *London Bridge* from the volume, and
he never again wanted to remember that he had written
it. He discarded this masterpiece from his work, he who
was one day to ransack his papers for the least scrap of
verse. What was the reason for this provisional and then
final exclusion? Because it was to Rimbaud that Verlaine
had determined to dedicate *Romances sans paroles,* because
it was in order to be taken into Rimbaud's favour again,
after the second of their separations in London and
before their reconciliation at Bouillon in May, 1873, that
he arranged the sequence of the poems in the volume—
a volume which was doubly Machiavellian, since it was

also constructed so as to serve equally well as his defence
in the suit for separation. Why? Because, but for the
Brussels drama, the volume would have appeared with
the dedication to Rimbaud. That accounts for the
provisional exclusion. And *London Bridge*, even after the
Brussels drama, was to remain excluded from the
Romances sans paroles, and then from all the rest of
Verlaine's volumes, because the poem is a condemnation
of his friendship for Rimbaud and amounts to a betrayal
of his memory: "I am going back to Rimbaud, if he
will have anything more to do with me after this betrayal you have made me commit"—as he wrote in the
letter from Quiévrain.

This is touching on the metaphysic, not merely of
homosexuality, but of friendship, since in its less gross
manifestations (and Heaven knows there are gross,
filthy ones, as may be seen in *Hombres!*) homosexuality
is the consequence of immeasurable friendship, of a
friendship which is absolute and incapable of distinguish-
ing soul from body, in the friend:

> Friendship, how divine it is between man and
> woman!

Verlaine exclaims in the first line of a sonnet in *Bonheur*,
hastening to add that "it does not inhibit any of the
necessary relationships." But the friendship between
man and woman is not suitable for creatures like Verlaine, constructed so essentially for friendship that they
cannot but confuse it with love and in love:

> There is nothing nobler in ancient or modern story,
> nothing more beautiful, than two friends.

For a cerebral erotic such as he was, a woman, unless she were a Staël or a George Sand, if then! could only satisfy his physical desire. But Mathilde was not a George Sand or a Staël, far from it. She was adequate for the contacts of the flesh, but not of the mind. The physical excitement over, she was incapable of interesting the man of letters that Verlaine was to the marrow, and was all his life, even when in the grip of absinthe; the æsthetic theorist who constantly needed some one to argue with him or listen to him. Yes, I doubt if any of the great French poets was more passionately interested in literary matters than Pauvre Lélian, more consistently a man of letters; in the midst of his conversion, even, the rage for writing affected him as forcibly as ever. Lepelletier, though no doubt too sceptical as to the profundity of this conversion, is not altogether wrong when he asserts that Verlaine envisaged it mainly as a theme for beautiful and fresh creations. In his passion for Rimbaud, the greatest and most lasting passion of his life and which, when Rimbaud died, was to wring a few beautiful strains from his senile genius, poetic admiration played a great part; those "mysterious delicacies" which he attributes to the adolescent Satan were certainly of the intellectual order. See how he links the epithet "learned" to Sodom and at the same time brands the unfortunate Mathilde with "stupid."

So, immediately he was released from Mons, it was to Rimbaud that Verlaine's thoughts turned. He had no doubt in his mind that Rimbaud, whose character he understood nothing whatever about (as the former makes him admit in *Une Saison en Enfer*), would come back to him. And besides, our neophyte was obsessed and on fire with the intention of converting that savage enemy of God. What an exemplary life they would lead together, their friendship purified, chastity and tranquillity assured by religion, in that England where piety and discipline (two warders lacking in atheistic and anarchistic France) are so firmly established! What magnificent philosophic and æsthetic arguments they would have, in the open-air, on their walks. And there would be no drinking, no going to public houses, only a glass of beer, though in any case sobriety such as theirs had nothing to be afraid of. And how submissive they would be to the religion of the London Sunday, and its prohibitions, their bug-bear in the old days!

That is why, after a heavy preparatory bombardment by letter already begun from Mons, Verlaine launched his offensive by going to see Rimbaud at Stuttgart, in February. We know the result of this journey, and how the attempted reconciliation and conversion culminated in a brawl from which *le Loyola* (the nickname with which the ex-Satanic Bridegroom henceforward favours the ex-Foolish Virgin) did not escape without some damage. Thanks to this episode, the tamest period in the poet's Bohemianism is not without its Saturnian tinge. M. Delahaye, who was in the confidence of both the antagonists, has told the story so well that we must give it in his description:

> And there a long and heated argument took place between these two "ideas" which was not, to use one of Verlaine's favourite expressions, *dans un sac*, seeing that it ran its course in many public-houses and came to an end, all arguments being exhausted, in a battle in which fists replaced words, on the very bank of the Neckar, whose moonlit water seemed to

offer these two madmen an only too natural epilogue
to their fantastic story.   They were in complete
solitude, there was no witness of the struggle, only
the phantom mass of the pines of the Black Forest
on the horizon. . . Very luckily the combatants had
neither knives nor revolvers, not even a stick.
Though he was the taller and the more robust,
Rimbaud soon realised that the other's delirium was
dangerous.   Verlaine, supple, sinewy, over-excited
with drink, was mad with rage, humiliation and
despair, believing himself irretrievably relapsed
after eighteen months of virtue and conquered by
Satan in spite of it all.   He wanted to strike, to be
struck, to go on struggling there for ever. . . He
fell exhausted at last and lay fainting on the bank,
whilst Rimbaud, damaged himself, made his way
back to the town as best he could.

At daybreak, on ground that had been torn up
by their struggling feet, some peasants found a man
lying half-dead. . .

So Verlaine had to go back to his dear Albion alone;
and many months as well as the most brutal rebuffs were
necessary before he would give up the attempt to regain
his lost friend, though not the hope of doing so.   In this
matter, though, circumstances were very much more
favourable to him than if he had won the day.   Deprived
of his dangerous companion, Pauvre Lélian was able to
enjoy the benefits of his penitentiary treatment.   As a
master at the school of a Mr. Andrews at Stickney, near
Boston, Lincolnshire, with board in lieu of salary, he
lived eighteen months in peace and sobriety, the best
months of his adult life, by a long way, he was to say

later. This lasted from March 1875 till September 1876 punctuated with quiet holidays at Arras, where his good mother had settled. It was at this time that he put the finishing touches to many of the poems in *Sagesse*, at this time that he composed several of the best poems in *Amour*. Then, having failed in his attempt to fly with his own pedagogic wings at Boston, by giving lessons at his home, he spent another year at Remington's School, Bournemouth, and those twelve months, too, were favourable to his health and his poetry:

> The long pine-wood winds down to the shore, the narrow wood of pine, laurel and fir, with the town in the midst of it, looking like a village, scattered houses red among the leafage and the white villas down on the beach. . . On the left rises the tower, it awaits a spire, of a church that is invisible from here. . . From the Protestant tower a peal of bells rings out; then two or three and four and then eight at once, an instinctive harmony, now far, now near. Enthusiasm, joy, appeal, sorrow, reproach, with gold and bronze and fire, are in that voice, that vast yet gentle sound the wood is listening to! Music is not more beautiful. . .

No, not more beautiful than such a poem, and this masterpiece is dated January 1877, in *Amour*. He was still to be found at Bournemouth in September, but by this time, however, the influence of Saturn was urging him to go back to France. "I have in my pocket," he announced to Lepelletier on the 7th, "two splendid English certificates with a visa from the local authorities, authenticated by the French Consulate-General in London."

Delahaye, himself wandering schoolmaster, but one whose peregrinations were confined to his own country, had just left the school of Notre-Dame, at Rethel, where he had been teaching for two years. Verlaine took his friend's place there in October 1877. He was to remain there for the two school-years, 77-78, 78-79, and it was during that time that the desire for alcohol again overcame him and that his passionate attachment to one of his pupils, Lucien Létinois, completed his fresh subjection to Saturn.

II. LUCIEN LÉTINOIS

At the end of July 1879 Pauvre Lélian, whose renewed intemperance made it scarcely possible for him to continue to carry out his duties, gave in his resignation, not much to the regret of the school authorities (Note 16). Lucien Létinois, who was approaching his twentieth year (he had been born on February 2nd, 1860), and had just failed in his leaving certificate examination, had no reason for staying on at the school, where his presence, undoubtedly, had been the cause of Verlaine's staying there so long. And the two of them made off to England.

This is an important episode in Verlaine's life which neither Lepelletier nor Delahaye knew about, or at least they had only a suspicion that it took place, without being able to agree as to the date or the circumstances. They do not place it before the farming partnership between Verlaine and Lucien's father, but one of them says that it was in the course of this partnership and the other at its conclusion. And they fill in the interval before the partnership by making the poet live at Coulommes, with the Letinois; which is really equiva-

I

lent to dating it August 1879. And they make the visit
to England one of very short duration. But might not
teacher and pupil have been to England twice together?
That is not impossible, according to Delahaye's version;
Lepelletier's is not worth consideration. What is certain
is that they were there on one occasion dating from
August 1879, and that no biographer has noticed it
before. Yet the fact was common knowledge, as it
could not have failed to be, to everyone in Coulommes;
the present writer collected the echoes of it on the very
spot and at a time when memories were fresher and the
witnesses more numerous than to-day (Note 17).

> I knew this child, my worry and delight, at a pious
> school in which I was a teacher. The slim and in-
> tractable youthfulness of seventeen, his real intelli-
> gence and the beautiful purity reflected in his eyes,
> his movements, his voice, captivated my heart and
> decided my choice of him for a son, since my true
> son, the son of my loins, was kept from me. . . I
> told him of my plan, to which he consented. He
> had parents whom he loved, whom he left in spirit
> to be mine. . .

This is the information given us in the poem numbered
xv in the section of *Amour* entitled "Lucien Létinois."
The first part quoted dates back to the moment of
Verlaine's arrival at Rethel (in October 1877 Lucien was
seventeen and a half); and the last to the time of his
leaving there. The boy left his parents in spirit and he
left them in the flesh from August 1879 till the beginning
of 1880. The obscure Poem VIII in the same section refers
to the Christmas of 1879, which they spent together in
London :

Oh, the horrible gloom on the happiest day of the year, in that monstrous city where our destiny was decided.

But with or without Lucien, Verlaine was living in England at the end of 1879, that is beyond doubt. He had carefully kept this visit secret, but he revealed it in a general account of his English school-mastering published in July 1894 by the *Fortnightly Review*, with the title: *Notes on England. Myself as a French Master.* This revelation, having been published in England, remained unnoticed till 1918, when M. G.-Jean Aubry made use of it in his interesting study, *Paul Verlaine at l'Angleterre.*

In that article the poet informs us that on leaving Rethel he went as a teacher of French to a school kept by a Mr. Murdoch at Lymington, a small town in Hampshire near Bournemouth, and opposite the Isle of Wight. Being in the New Forest, Lymington is surrounded by woods. Verlaine had in his charge, at least to take out for walks, thirty pupils, he says, of whom two were French:

> Every day we used to go for a walk of an hour or two in the woods nearby; there we used regularly to meet the girls from a neighbouring boarding-school in charge of a French school-mistress. It was very romantic.

This enables us to understand why Poem XXIII in "Lucien Létinois" was written, an impenetrable mystery until the *Notes on England* had been made public:

> Oh, the New Forest! that name evocative of faery and of battles. Often the musket shattered love-

spells and enchantments under your boughs and
terrified their nightingales. Oh, Shakespeare; Oh,
Cromwell, Oh, the New Forest! Now the name is
lovely only, no longer tragic nor magic, but with
delightful logic framing the old town of Lymington,
the oldest and most lovely of those once warrior-
towns, in a rim of numberless trees proud of their
lofty grace, with the sea dreaming aloud not far off,
like a powerful echo of the things of the past. I
lived there alone, or almost alone, for several
months; alone and secluded. . .

There is nothing in this poem, any more than there
is in the narrative in the *Fortnightly*, to indicate Lucien's
presence in Lymington or the vicinity. But in the poem
he does appear as the writer of a series of letters inspired
by "a filial love with a sacred thrill":

Sacred, surely.—Oh, his letters in the week, in the
glazed box, and that I took out with me on my
walk through the woods, mad, mad with joy, re-
reading them a hundred times. . .

This correspondance is undoubtedly the same as that
with which Poem VI of "Lucien Létinois" is wholly
concerned:

Oh, his letters of that time, and mine too. I do not
believe there could be anything to surpass them . . .
But his! his letters! the angel ignorant of our ways,
the pure spirit clad in innocent flesh!
Oh, memory, the dearest to me, perhaps, of all!
Clear words, child's phrases, the chaste and simple
style where virtue dwelt. . . . .

and it presupposes a separation. Having this poem, we cannot think, as otherwise it would have been natural to do, that Lucien was one of the two French pupils Verlaine mentions. Indeed, it seems almost as if we must conclude that whilst his schoolmaster was at Lymington Lucien remained at Coulommes.

Let us look closer, though. We shall see that in Poems XXIII and VI the word "separation" is not mentioned nor is the idea expressed, apart from the fact of there being this correspondence. Now, would not Verlaine, parted from Lucien at the highest pitch of the passion that enflamed him, have sighed and eloquently deplored the pains of absence, he who has told us of his "rage of loving" in reference to this very boy? We must ask, too, if it is conceivable that at the height of this love, which was "almost fleshly in its loving care," Pauvre Lélian would have been capable of living happily for several months without the frequent and neighbouring presence of the beloved person, if not with his close and constant company.

As to the correspondence so belauded by these two poems, we find by examining Poem VI that it was something quite out of the ordinary; it was not meant for the exchange of news and emotions in the usual way, but for the exchange of thoughts written by two people within reach of one another, even seeing each other frequently, but who wished to converse in writing on matters too deep and too delicate to be discussed by word of mouth; who wished also to avoid arousing the suspicions of those about them by a too-pronounced intimacy. If Poem VI does not authorise the second supposition, which springs from the peculiar situation the two friends were in, it certainly calls for the first:

Oh, his letters of that time and mine too! I do not think anything can surpass them. I was, I cannot say better, truly good, or rather, to say everything, truly Christian. I was filled with wisdom and solicitude, expending all my pious care, all the devotion my being was capable of, to confirm that soul in the practice of prayer and love.

It is a spiritual director who is writing there, a Christian encouragement that he is giving and that he receives in his turn:

But his letters, his! the angel ignorant of our ways! . . . and such an exchange implies, we repeat, presence rather than separation. Daily presence? Weekly, more probably, if we take account of, "Oh, his letters *in the week*," and of, "I lived there alone, or almost alone."

Was Lucien living in Lymington at some other school than Murdoch's? Was he lodging with some family in the town and attending the school as a day-scholar; though, as he was now approaching twenty he is not likely to have done that? Perhaps he was at the school as an usher, or living in the neighbourhood, in Bournemouth, for example, at some school where Verlaine had formerly taught. All these hypotheses are plausible. But even if he were living in Lymington, even if a boarder at Murdoch's, they could not have been together all the time, for Verlaine would have had his duties to perform, and Lucien, too, if he did have some employment there; and prudence would have advised against it, too; they could only really have had each other's company on Sundays. During the week they would have had to be content with letters:

Oh, his letters in the week, *in the glass-backed letter-box.* . .

Does it not seem as if this letter-box dispensed with the services of the postman? If, at Lymington, Lucien, a pupil at the school or living outside, used to come *during the week* to put his letters in this glass-backed box, which was the receptacle for private as well as for postal correspondence, and, supposing him to have been an usher, taking Verlaine's missives from the same box, what would there have been strange in that after what happened in Guernsey? For did not the greatest of poets and the most faithful of mistresses, who spent half of each day together, still feel the need to carry on a daily correspondence over a space of years with the aid of a similar letter-box?

But did the correspondence to which Poems vi and xxiii refer really take place with the regularity these poems would have us believe? Was it not in part created by the poet's imagination, by the desire to place under the safeguard of religion this more than disquieting attachment, to sanctify a friendship which might be considered more than profane? One must be prepared for everything when dealing with a man who was at once so calculating and so unconscious and, not to mince matters, so demented. His desire to remain enigmatic, to write so as to be understood only by himself, is obvious in these two poems. It was impossible for a poet with his mania for confession to be silent about his stay at Lymington, and he even had to admit that there he was only *almost alone*. But he managed, even though he blabbed, to avoid making himself understood; and without his *Notes on England* we should still be completely in the dark as to his meaning.

His anxiety to remain mysterious and full of reticence about his stay in England with Lucien is evident again in

Poem VIII of the same section, very much more difficult
to write than the other two had been, but to the execution
of which he was impelled by a force stronger than his
will:

> Oh, the hateful gloom on the gayest day of the
> year, in the monstrous city where our destiny was
> decided!*

He had shifted his quarters, but with such precautions that Delahaye, not to mention Lepelletier, was
completely deceived as to the date of the scene to which
this poem refers, as we shall see later. It took place in
London, at Christmas 1879, when this dangerous
adoptive father, followed by his unfortunate offspring,
had left Mr. Murdoch's morally protective roof. And
with what result? I leave it to the reader's judgment.
Pass this over, psychologist, or, rather, since it is your
function to probe, probe no deeper than is necessary. . .

III. THE EXPERIMENT IN FARMING

After this anglo-pedagogic preamble, and his fate with
Lucien having been decided on that Christmas Day of
1879, the period of Pauvre Lélian's rural Bohemianism
begins. This was to take him up to the summer of 1885.

---

*I add the three stanzas that follow to make the argument clearer:(T)
Instead of the expected happiness, what deep grief, what
shadows! I was like a dead man and you were immersed in
sombre thoughts.
   The darkness deepened as the day advanced, outside our
window as in our souls, like a pure, a sublime love clasped by
some infamous lust.
   And the fearful fog flowed on, even into our room, where
the candle seemed a silent reproach, as on the morrow of
some orgy. . .

The drama was played on two country stages and was divided into three acts, the second and third being separated by an interval spent in Paris.

The first act was set at Coulommes, in the arrondissement of Vouziers and lasted from January to March 1880, the 18th March being the date when our agriculturalist notified the Juniville police of his change of residence (Note 18). Juniville, in the arrondissement of Rethel, about eleven miles from Coulommes, was the scene of the second act, which ended in the middle of 1882. The third began in the middle of 1883 and was again at Coulommes. In the interval "the Englishman of Coulommes," as he had been called in the district since his return with Lucien, went back to Paris for a short rehearsal, a perfectly representative one, of the last phase of his Bohemianism.

The parents of Lucien Létinois were living at Coulommes at the time when their boy, a boarder at the school of Notre-Dame at Rethel, met Verlaine. They supported themselves there with difficulty on a small bit of land.

Their penuriousness explains why this courageous peasant couple, already advanced in years, should have fallen in so easily with the project Verlaine laid before them. Though a persuasive talker, and himself convinced of what he was saying, it was not merely his eloquence fortified by this conviction that they were beguiled by. He had all the prestige that attached to a master from the most respected ecclesiastical school in the neighbourhood, coupled with the prestige of money. If they represented poverty, he was wealth. The visit to England to which he had just treated Lucien was sufficient to show them that his finances were in good order;

but this amiable gentleman who seemed to have dropped among them from heaven, whose conversation was all piety, brought positive proofs to satisfy their matter-of-factness. Verlaine, whose free and easy existence till that time had been not one of wealth but of comfort, was at this actual moment, rich. From the poor woman whom he had plundered unmercifully since her widow-hood of small and larger sums, he had just extracted a very considerable amount, representing his share of his father's property—which share, though, he had really devoured, and drunk, several times over already. This sum was large enough to enable him to pay thirty thousand francs for a farm at Juniville (the amount given in the conveyance, and very likely undervalued), and not to have to economise on the expenses of installation, let alone those preceding it. The Létinois believed that Verlaine was really wealthy, and in abandoning the meagre property on which they were vegetating they were not letting go of the substance for the shadow, for Verlaine put the purchase in the name of Lucien's father (under the protection, I imagine, of a defeasance of which the old peasant would not see the danger).

In this, however, the poet, as his custom was, combined the ingenuous with the crafty. He adored this youth whom Providence had planted like an oasis in the insupportable wilderness through which his rage for love was passing. He saw him through the haze of the most visionary imagination. Thanks to this child and his excellent father and mother, Verlaine, derelict though he was, would reach port, and, relaunched, with the ensign of happiness at the stern, sail across a stormless sea. No more Bohemianism, a home, but secure and blessed in a way that that other home in which a bad marriage had landed him had not been.   On his adopted child (for he had quite made up his mind, unfamiliar as he was with the law, to adopt Lucien; though in fact he could not possibly have done so), he would shower all the treasures of a paternal sensibility, all those riches of which his lawful son was deprived through his wife's spite and her parents' baseness.   And his blessed mother, robbed of her lawful descendant, would find compensation in this adopted grandchild, a paragon of beauty, health, intelligence, affection and piety.   And through all this, Pauvre Lelian, who had been born by the decree of Saturn

> the child of great cities and of slavish revolts,

poisoned by their civilisation and anti-natural claims, would be restored to the life of the soil from which he had sprung.   In place of an atmosphere noxious both to his health and his poetic gift, he would breathe the good smell of the ploughed land; and inspired by Nature and with the support of a loving God, he would be able to give to Poetry those works that the soul of France needed for her regeneration.   And how could he possibly not stop drinking?   Is there time to drink when you are growing corn?

> This is the festival of the corn, the festival of bread!

Thus his aimless, guideless existence would follow the path of charity, self-devotion, and sanctity to a Christian death:

> The little home, the little nest that I have found,
> and the great hopes that I have nursed, may God's

blessing be upon them. The hours of past faults are erased from the pure dial of my thoughts.

Innocence surrounds me, and you, Simplicity. What can my heart lack, by Jesus visited? My poverty, my solitude, coarse bread, rough bed, such jealous care, exquisite devotion!

This devotion of the loving soul to the elected heart comes to give a tranquil and so refreshing conclusion to the distress of my life, still unsatiated for having satisfied every whim.

Thanks unto you, O Lord, is not this the Christian death? Love my patient effort and our struggles! Heaven sees us, me and mine, enter, Lord, by the humble road, into your Bliss.

But beneath these admirable sentiments less praiseworthy ones were hidden; sentiments that were certainly not inspired by Monsignor Gaume's catechism— that *Catéchisme de persévérance* the poet had always carried with him ever since it had brought about his conversion, the first time he read it, in the prison at Mons. Under the surface simpleton, "I who am all tenderness and artlessness, alas," may be glimpsed, may be seen plainly, the cunning plotter. Vexation at his widowerhood, rancour against Mathilde and her parents, were influences in his project of adopting Lucien, as well as in his giving away of the Juniville farm. There was the question, too, of continuing to avoid paying his wife, who, without means of her own, had charge of their child, the maintenance allowance the courts had ordered. By putting his property in the name of Lucien's father he would escape prosecution by the Mauté's, who, so he argued, would have served a writ on him, had it been in their son-in-law's name. It was with this admirable argument, evidently, that he overcame his feeble mother's hesitations, for she was not without the sense to know that the best way of preventing her son's money from being seized was for him not to take it from her, from her who kept it only for him. And the thirty or forty thousand francs which were going to be swallowed up in this absurd enterprise were yet the sole barrier protecting mother and son from ruin! How was it that Verlaine, however demented he may have been, did not appreciate that fact? He would probably have told us,

> To that I can only answer that truly I was born under Saturn.

But perhaps he said to himself, too, that his mother was no longer young, and that if she died the Mauté's would not leave her heir in peace.

If the experiment in farming came to a sad conclusion, do not let us, though, accuse old Létinois, as I see Delahaye does, of having, with peasant ambition, wished to increase the area of his farm. This hypothesis is not supported by any fact, and it is as gratuitous, if not as grave, as Lepelletier's affirmation which accuses the Létinois of having urged the poet to buy the Juniville property and then "lain in wait for his discomfiture," in order to "round off their land" at his cost. The truth is that both these biographers of Verlaine are ignorant, the first hardly less so than the second, of all that concerns the Juniville period; that they received no news of their friend during that period, and that having been obliged to have recourse to invention, the partiality of friendship urged them on, each according to his character—and Lepelletier is never remarkable for moderation. But at

least he does not paint us—as the good Delahaye is not
afraid to do—a picture of Verlaine getting down "very
resolutely" to the job; learning to "feed and groom the
horses and look after the sheep and cattle until the time
when he would be able to mow and plough."

At Juniville, Verlaine was like those birds of the air
and lilies of the field we are told about in the Gospels.
He sowed not, neither did he reap, but he was there, and
his presence was a drag on the farm that old Létinois,
stout-hearted though he might be, could not cope with.
Whilst the peasant bent over his tasks the poet was in bed,
out walking, at church, or at the public-house; and if the
capital expenses came out of his purse, as long as he had
one:

> Alas, all this happiness that I thought permitted me,
> . . . fell in ruins through money matters as a wall
> collapses. . .

a good part of the proceeds from the sale of the crops
passed down his throat, in solid and liquid form, for the
country air sharpens the appetite, and it turned out that
Mother Létinois was an excellent cook. But besides,
Verlaine was more intent on literature than ever, and he
passed no little time in the capital he had so abused, whilst
he found a publisher for *Sagesse* and saw it through the
press, in 1880-1; and not content with not putting his
shoulder to the wheel himself, he took Lucien away from
the work of the farm, after having attached him to it
by such stout hexameters:

> There I used to see your delicate outline against the
> sky, striding behind the plough with active steps,
> scolding at the horses, but rightly, without anger,
> and shouting gee-hup and gee-wo.

> I saw you harrowing and rolling, mowing
> sometimes, consulting the old men, anxious abou
> a cloud; in the winter threshing or binding faggots
> in our woods. I used to help you, soon out of
> breath and sweating.

He provided him with a buggy, in which they both used
to drive about the countryside and visit the inns. He
dressed him in the fashion, at least of Rethel or Reims,
if not of Paris. He paid the fifteen hundred francs for
him needed for a year's voluntary military service, gave
him pocket-money when he was with his regiment and,
when the young artilleryman was stationed at the neighbouring camp of Châlons, he visited him so frequently
that he soon rented a room from a canteen-keeper,
alleging that this would be less expensive than going
backwards and forwards.

> My son is brave. He rides on his war-horse. . .
> I still see you on your horse whilst the bugles were
> sounding. . .
> I see you amongst the guns. . .

His period of service over, Verlaine sent him to
London to perfect his English,—that is Delahaye's version, as promised above,

> Following the system most in use, the best, too, for
> making rapid progress, Lucien took mutual lessons
> (French lessons, English in exchange). Among his
> pupils there was a young lady who became very
> friendly with him, in a sisterly way at first, but
> threatening to turn into a quite different emotion.
> Létinois was to blame, no doubt, to some extent.

The robust young countryman, with simple rustic gaiety, became on more familiar terms with his pupil than was right. . . In short, one day the poor boy saw the day approaching when his robust peasant's blood would get the better of his virtue. He wrote to Verlaine, confessed, admitted his temptations, his fears. The distracted father takes train and boat and snatches "his child" away from perfidious Albion. It is to his arrival in London on New Year's Day that Poem VIII of *Lucien Létinois* alludes.

What is all this based on? Not on anything solid. The letters referred to in Poem VI? But even if we did not know what we have learnt from *Notes on England*, that poem tells us Lucien's age:

Twenty years old! Three years afterwards he was born into eternal glory, filling my memory for ever!

But it was not after his year of military service that Lucien was twenty, but at the end of 1879 or the beginning of 1880; his death, three years afterwards, took place in 1883. Is it Poem VIII that Delahaye has in mind? Even allowing, as he wishes, that "the gayest day of the year" refers to New Year's Day and not to Christmas Day, how can we believe that the moment that decided the "fate" of the two friends was placed so late in the development of their relations? Delahaye's imagination has certainly been misled by the position of Poem VIII in *Lucien Létinois* where it follows one referring to Lucien's military service ("My son is brave, he rides on his war-horse"), and containing this stanza:

My son is good: one day when the suspicion of a
fault reached my ears, my child, foreseeing my
paternal anguish, came to console me with his noble
avowals.

The different poems in *Lucien Létinois*, however, are far
from being arranged in chronological order, for if they
were, the poem relating to the stay at Lymington would
not be the twenty-third in a series of twenty-five. And
if the fault alluded to in this stanza was really of the kind
our biographer believes, if there was really a feminine
snake in the garden, why situate it in London? Poem VII
seems to refer to the fault of an artillery man rather than
of a student of languages. And then it is the guilty person
who "comes to console"; there is no mention of going
to him and crossing the Channel.

So many expenses (apart from those necessitated by
Lucien's second visit to England, if it took place) were
paid for in really priceless poetic currency by the magnificent poems in *Amour*, where the poet evokes the
beloved who has passed away, but they did not help
Lucien's father and mother to escape from the difficulties
which were submerging them. In 1882 (I cannot date it
more closely), pursued by creditors whom his financial
backer could not satisfy, old Létinois lost his head, and
the whole family, including Lucien, took refuge in
Belgium. Verlaine sold up the farm and rescued some
fifteen thousand francs, which he returned to his mother
(so Delahaye tells us, who, however, does not mention
the Létinois's flight into Belgium). Then the fugitives
left Belgium and, not daring to return to live at Coulommes, sought shelter in Paris, in the Chapelle district,
where Verlaine rejoined them. There is nothing to be

K

relied on in Lepelletier's narrative, who makes old
Létinois "sell off the farm to his own advantage, naturally" (we shall refer to this again), and sends Verlaine
and Lucien to London to forget their "agricultural
disappointments."

How many weeks was it after the combined house-
holds had settled down in Paris that Lucien took up the
post, that Delahaye had got for him, of teacher or usher
at a private school at Boulogne-sur-Seine? The biographer gives us no indication. Lucien stayed there two
months, only long enough to find "a position in an
industrial establishment" (that Delahaye does not specify)
"which was better paid and more suited to his tastes and
aptitudes than the other."

Verlaine took Lucien's place at the school, and as there
were plenty of furnished rooms at Boulogne, he took
one there at 5 rue de Parchamps. He published some
portions of his *Mémoires d'un Veuf* in papers to which
Lepelletier (with whom he had renewed a correspondence interrupted for five years) introduced him, and
at the same time he nursed the hope of being speedily
re-admitted to his old job at the Hôtel de Ville, a hope in
which Lepelletier, who had taken the matter up for him,
encouraged him. The faithful Lucien used to come and
see him by the railway which runs round the outskirts of
Paris, and Verlaine would meet him at the station:

> My friend, do you in the heart of Paradise, remem-
> ber the station at Auteuil and the train which used
> to bring you from Chapelle every day, long ago?
> Long ago, already! Yet how I remember my vigils
> at the foot of the steep stairway, waiting for you;
> and unforgettable your gracefulness coming down

those stairs, slim and light-moving as one of the
angels on Jacob's Ladder,

. . . every day, at first; then when the Létinois had moved
to Ivry, no doubt because Lucien had found employment there, every Sunday. They used to lunch at the
Hotel Coutret, where Verlaine had established his head-
quarters, then go for a walk in the Bois:

My poor child, your voice in the Bois de Boulogne!

and afterwards the poet would return alone to his
furnished room. But so much leisure and loneliness were
not to be endured without an accompaniment the nature
of which may be guessed. What with aperitifs and what
with liqueurs, "the nervous system becomes exas-
perated," Delahaye remarks. The drinker succumbed
to morbid depression and at times saw red, when
Mathilde and "that old . . . Mauté" came into his mind,
as he says in a letter to Lepelletier, of January 9th, 1883.
He appealed to his mother, she rushed to him, nursed
him, then went back to her peaceful lodgings at Arras,
where he rejoined her and from which he dislodged her.
For as his re-admission to the Hotel de Ville could not
possibly be long delayed, why should they wait before
settling down in Paris again? They moved to lodgings,
already very humble ones, alas! in the rue Roquette; and
here the poets of the advance guard used to come to pay
homage to the author of *Sagesse*, the masterpiece that had
been obscurely published some eighteen months before,
but to which the literary groups were beginning to pay
attention. And the literary cafés of the Latin Quarter
welcomed with open arms the man whom they had
driven away, in company with Rimbaud, ten years

before; that very Rimbaud for whom Verlaine gained their applause when he recited poems of his which he remembered.

Hirsutes and Hydropathes: in their "cellars" there was no less drinking than at the meetings of the Vilains-Bonshommes in 1872, and the poor mother was the witness of the active recrudescence of a drunkenness which was sometimes, often, the cause of her being treated with none of the consideration that was her due. Weeks of drunken bouts were followed by weeks of conversion, and in the midst of it all Lucien Létinois was carried off by typhoid fever, and then the funeral procession from the Hospice de la Pitié to the Ivry cemetery. . .

Ivry, the terrible devourer, has your remains under its sod. Beneath colourless and scentless flowers and stunted, unmysterious trees.

VAGABONDAGE

VI.   VAGABONDAGE

I.   THE ENGLISHMAN OF COULOMMES

To think that the Muses constitute a Providence which, though not determining the fate of their children, intervenes when the events have occurred, and, like a wise liquidator, utilises for poetic ends the catastrophes the poets have suffered—this is a belief to which the life story of more than one poet lends credence. But none so much as the life-story of Verlaine; could there have been any other reason for the four years he has just passed through except that they should provide him with the material for that volume, *Amour*, in which faith and grief, misfortune and resignation have raised him to a level the summits of which are equal to his highest achievements?   In this volume the twenty-five poems which make up a wreath laid on the tomb of Lucien Létinois are quite the most affecting elegies for a friendship cut short by death that French poetry has produced. But the poet's tears, though wept for his friend, are wept for himself too; they are prophets of the abominable fate that awaits him like a condemned prisoner who has been refused a reprieve.

For the loss of Lucien Létinois meant to Verlaine the loss of his religious feeling as well.   It was not to fade before it had set his whole being aflame, and the Christian sentiments expressed have a magnificent passion, but it was fire which for lack of fuel was to die out as swiftly and naturally as it had blazed up.

151

My son is dead. I worship your will, Oh my God,
and I offer you the tears of a heart which had almost
been false to its vow. . .
Your chastisement is severe, my son is dead, alas! . . .
You had given him me, you take him from me
again, Glory be yours!

"You had given him me" at that moment of crisis when,
as the most beautiful poem in *Bonheur* tells us:

    . . . like a foundering ship I was about to plunge my
flesh in the sombre waters of debauchery, my flesh
and my once conquering spirit,

and "you take him from me again" when

    . . . my poor weary feet cried out for this beloved
guide in that narrow path. Glory be yours!

Alas! this hosannah was a farewell. What was his
Christian Muse to give us after this? Little, indeed; only,
in *Bonheur* and *Liturgies intimes*, the chips that had fallen
under the work-bench whilst he was constructing *Sagesse*
and *Amour*. What genius he had left he was to employ
in the service of a Muse as profane as his dead Muse had
been sacred; he was to give us *Parallèlement*, of which but
few pieces, fortunately, remained to be written. As a
great poet he had played out his part.

If he brought it to an end so successfully, it was because
an interval of sobriety followed the loss of Lucien. But
soon the truth of the maxim that he who has once gone
back to drink will go back to it again was affirmed with a
violence which avenged the pains of abstinence. From
the early months of 1884 onwards, Pauvre Lélian no

longer attempts to drown his sorrows in religion alone,
but in drink, and in absinthe of all drinks, a drink which
till then he had given up, if not completely, at least, to
use his own expression, "practically," believing that it
had been responsible for his attack on Rimbaud. But
now he was to be deep in the lakes of the green witch
until the day when,

Woman should have quite dominated him again.

How was he ever to drag himself out of an abyss where
even his mother's supplications were powerless to prevent him, if only for a moment, from plunging? Yet
they both sought the means of saving him. There was
only one solution of the problem. Paul, whose health
was just then attacked for the first time by his arthritis,
could never be rescued if he stayed in Paris. It was essential to get him away from the literary atmosphere where
he could not go a yard without drinking, for he had his
own seat in the cafés. With the few thousand francs they
had left, and the wad was dwindling terrifyingly day by
day, they must settle down in the country. Only there
would it be possible to get pure air and practice sobriety
and economy.

The Létinois' house at Coulommes was empty and
the Verlaines bought it. And even before the contract
was completed they rushed to live there, for there was no
time to be lost. The agreement was drawn up in the
office of the family solicitor—a witness, oh, shame and
remorse, of their old prosperity—Maître Sabot, at Batignolles, Paris, on July 30th and 31st, 1883. It was completed for the sum of three thousand five hundred francs,
paid in cash, with immediate possession. The property
was situated at a place called Malval (how Saturnian a

name, and notice that just before Saturn had lodged them
in a street called la Roquette). It comprised "a dwelling-
house, outhouses, courtyard and garden amounting to a
quarter of an acre." Purchaser: "Dame Stéphanie-
Julie-Josèphe Dehée, independent, widow of the late
Nicolas-Auguste Verlaine, late of 17 rue de la Roquette,
Paris, at present of Coulommes." Vendor: "Jean
Baptiste Létinois, independent, and Dame Marie-Louise-
Delphine Moreaux, his wife, living at 14 rue de Paris,
Ivry, Seine."

Was this a way of forcing Létinois to reimburse a part
of the sum he had appropriated out of the sale of the
Juniville farm? That is what Lepelletier insinuates, with
that malevolence towards the other party characteristic
of the lawyer when he sets out to prove that black is
white. "This sly peasant had, on the death of his son,
sold the house mentioned without handing over the sum
realised to its true owners, it seems." This "it seems,"
changed into direct affirmation by biographers at second
hand (Note 19), is, as it is, a glaring falsity, since Juniville
was sold at the time of the catastrophe; sold by Verlaine
himself and without any intervention from Létinois.
The rehabilitation of this poor devil, the victim of the
poet's madness, is, I believe, an act of justice reserved for
the historian who shall give us that accurate account of
the Juniville-Coulommes period that Verlaine's biography
is still in need of. But as far as the purchase of Coulommes
is concerned, that looks more like the exploitation of the
peasant by the poet than the reverse.

Lepelletier was the more careless because Verlaine
told him in a letter, of November 28th, 1887 (to which
we shall refer again), that he was impatiently awaiting
the repayment of a debt: "I will explain; it is with a solici-

tor, Maître Corette, at Juniville (Ardennes) and is, I believe, the remains of a' deposit in guarantee of payment for some property sold by me in 1882." Several times, besides, in his letters and in his work, there is proof that Juniville was sold by Verlaine and for his benefit solely —though unfortunately only a nominal benefit, once the farm's creditors had been paid off. There is the fact, too, that Verlaine, who was always ready to make complaints, however fantastically he may have handled his affairs, never made the least complaint against the Létinois; we have Delahaye's own word for it, who knew the Létinois and their son well, in Paris.

Let us at the same time clear the inhabitants of Coulommes of the reproach that Delahaye hints at—that they gave Verlaine a very cold welcome for no reason at all and unjustly ostracized him. For the catastrophes that Pauvre Lélian and his more pitiable mother were subjected to without respite let us make Saturn responsible; that will suffice.

Arrived at Coulommes, Verlaine did exactly what he would have done if he had remained in Paris, only, perhaps, he came to it more quickly. With nothing to do, apart from his literary preoccupations, which did not oblige him to keep sober, deprived of all companionship in the slightest degree intellectual . . . or moral, he hurried towards that condition bordering on delirium tremens mentioned in Mathilde's petition and Rimbaud's depositions. Not content with enriching the publicans with the pence he extorted with threats from his seventy-five year old mother, he made their house, in the place called Malval, the rowdy resort of all the louts of the district, and added a few more blackbirds to the *mille e tre* of his heretical youth. This did not happen without their plucking him, often with his consent and sometimes without it. One of them he fitted out with a merry-go-round outfit at a cost of fifteen hundred francs (the same amount as he had paid for Lucien's year of volunteer service). Two others, late one night, waited for him to come out of an inn, tumbled him into a ditch and emptied his pockets. They were arrested on his charge and sentenced at the Vouziers police-court, but in view of their youth and the special circumstances of the offence, their punishment was a light one. This incident is not recorded by Verlaine's biographers, but a letter of his to Léon Vanier, dated November 4th, 1884, proves its authenticity, though details are lacking: "Forced to wait, through being a witness in a case of theft of which I was the victim, till they condescend to call me, in person, here I have to stick." *Parallèlement* does not give us any information about this episode, but it helps us to realise that it did take place:

> It was quaint and must have made Satan laugh, that summer day had made me quite drunk! And that indescribable singer and all the stuff she came out with! . . .
> I had been roaming among the drink-shops such as you get in these little towns, not shifting much booze. Three urchins with perverted eyes kept on staring at my mug most unmannerly.
> These little louts openly hooted at me not far from the station. I gave them such a mighty telling-off that I very nearly swallowed my cigar.

This *Poème saturnien* springs from the same stock as the poem "On a Reliquary that was Stolen from him," that may be read in *Amour*. For Verlaine was almost as

assiduous an attendant at Mass and Vespers as at the
public-houses; and this Loyolaesque combination did
not render the inhabitants of Coulommes any more
respectful than the Rimbaud of Stuttgart had been, ten
years before, when he wrote: "Verlaine arrived here the
other day with a rosary in his paws. . . Three hours later
he had denied his God and made Our Saviour's ninety-
eight wounds bleed afresh." But the poet had not that
wealth of indulgence for the people of Coulommes that
he always retained for his one-time companion in hell. So
he called on the "great Saint Benoît Labre" (whose
squalid ways he only too closely espoused) to witness his
shame at having to live

> among these hypocritical peasants who are enough
> to disgust you with being alive, a crowd of Onans
> and Potiphars,

whose confusion between mine and thine relegated
them "to the level of the obscene."

II. THE TRAMP

Is there a last degree of alcoholic degradation? If so,
how far off it was this unfortunate man a year and a half
after having settled at Coulommes? Had he not, in the
interval, induced his mother to make over to him as a
gift the house that shéltered them? (The deed was signed
at Maître Chartier's, solicitor, at Attigny, April 17th,
1884.) That sheltered them . . . him, but soon her no
longer; for the fear that her son and her son's crapulous
friends caused her, and the spectacle he presented, in the
end drove her away. She had been sheltered by neigh-

bours several times, by the Daves, a couple who kept a grocer's shop next door, and she definitely took refuge with them in January 1885; and, terrified, would not yield to the supplications and commands with which Verlaine assailed her. It was at the Daves' house that, on February 11th, after a whirlwind journey to Paris, that the demented man, furious because in his absence his mother, helped by the Daves, had forced her way into the house (to remove some clothes or things), committed the actual violence and uttered the threats against the unhappy woman which got him a month's imprisonment from the Vouziers justices on March 24th.

To this affair we owe a chapter in *Mes Prisons* which is more remarkable for its lively descriptions of the trial and its results than for its veracity about what are called "the facts of the case." "Did not some awful Belgians who had wormed their way into your confidence," the author says, addressing his mother's memory, "denounce me, after I had myself complained to the authorities at V . . . . of a 'rape of domicile' committed by the aforesaid Belgians, who, after having had fires at different places, were living at C . . . . in the Ardennes!"

V . . . . is Vouziers. C . . . . is Coulommes. The Daves were, in fact, Belgians. "Rape of domicile"; *violation* is the term, but "rape" has the more criminal sound, and the Daves' action cannot be too severely qualified. Pauvre Lélian shows more moderation where the charges against himself are concerned; he passes over the *violence*, the principal charge, and admits to the *menaces*, the secondary charge, but wording them thus: "If you do not come back, I shall kill myself," instead of "I shall kill you," as the Public Prosecutor charged him, though subsidiarily.

Lepelletier saw the official documents in the case; he allots several pages to the affair, but in that tendencious way exacted by his rôle as the "executor of Verlaine's moral will and testament," expressly charged by him, "to defend my reputation"; a rôle proclaimed in the preface to his book. He draws a veil over the principal charge, leaves the subsidiary one in the vague, and attributes motives to the Daves and the secondary witnesses which the documents (consulted by us) do not justify him in doing. Yet it would have been so simple, since his historian's scruples urged him to be copious about this "ever-to-be-regretted scene, which," he says, "I wish could be erased from Verlaine's life, and not be mentioned in this work, but which" . . . it would have been so simple to have contented himself with pleading extenuating circumstances, since he does plead them:

> . . . On February 9th, 1885, Verlaine came to Paris. He went to the English tavern, Fox Austin's Hotel, in the rue d'Amsterdam. The potent whisky and stout were in this instance, no doubt, his inducement to choose that place to stay at, which was out of the way of his usual neighbourhood. . . Perhaps he was ruminating the idea of returning to England, as his custom was, following domestic scenes and upsets. He was probably under the influence of drink when he left Coulommes. It is certain that he was out of his mind and had lost all sense of what was right when he left the English tavern, the next morning but one, to return to Coulommes.

To have confined himself to these facts would have been better than slandering the Daves for having shown kindness and courage, and who, besides, did not de-

nounce Verlaine except in answer to the charge of violation of domicile that he had brought against them. I
may add that the Daves (and not Danes, as Lepelletier
spells it, and, following him, all those who, on his word for
it, wax indignant against the defenders of the poet's poor
mother) have left an excellent reputation in the Attigny
district and that direct descendants of theirs, who have
taken French nationality, are still living at Coulommes.

But if "the hostility shown against him by the local
witnesses" was, as Lepelletier asserts, the principal cause
of the poet being found guilty, it had no effect on the
sentence passed on him which, as the devoted biographer
himself acknowledges, was very lenient (a quasi-acquittal
he calls it). But the contrite attitude of the accused was a
factor in this moderation shown in his favour. Verlaine,
in *Mes Prisons*, expressed his gratitude to his judges for
this. He acknowledged it at the time by not entering an
appeal; and when the interval allowed for an appeal had
expired he went to serve his sentence, which came to an
end on May 13th. On the 8th March, however, not less
pressed for money than La Fontaine's two companions,
he had sold the house in the place called Malval for a little
less than half the price his mother had paid for it. And
whilst she found shelter no one knows where, it was a
Bohemian without hearth or home that the prison at
Vouziers lodged.

A happy month. A month of sobriety in which Verlaine's muse was far from idle, yet still left her poet time
"to attend to his chores; to sweep and to dust," and to
play knuckle-bones with the head-warder when the day's
work was over; and to say his paternoster and ave maria
in the dormitory each night. This is attested by the
following letter, hitherto unpublished, I believe:

11th May (de Profundis)

My dear friend, when this reaches you I shall have returned to Coulommes, and I shall leave there next Monday for Paris. Will tell you my plans. You, on receipt of this, must write to me care of Courtois, letting me know where to find you in town during the day, or at what time in the evening at your home.

Verses enclosed, of which one sonnet was published long ago. The style shows that, doesn't it? I am weak enough to be fond of the language and construction, flat and unction-lacking, of the poem on the reliquary I had pinched.

Will *Lombes* amuse you? It makes part of a series that I am sending to the *Revue indépendante* by the same post, a vaguely audacious series that will please you, I think. I am giving *Lutèce* three poems; more fantasy about them, all by the same post, and I am writing to Vanier and to Courtois, too. To our speedy meeting then, and best wishes to you and yours,

Your P. V.

P.S.—Several *Mémoires d'un Veuf*. A very clear idea for a novel—very warm, lively and poetic. Outline of *Madame Aubin* fixed. Found pencil, as you see, and a little paper, rather late, but still. . .

This letter was in fact written in pencil and on a square of paper small enough to have escaped the jailer's vigilance, for it does not bear the prison stamp. Written two days before Verlaine's release, perhaps he thought he would be able to send it—following the immemorial custom, by the help of a fellow prisoner whose time was

L

up before his. But he did not do so; on May 13th it was
still in his possession, for it has these words jotted on it:
"Free, keep all the poems of *Amour* for me, especially,
'My son is dead'. . ."

This note is at the top of the piece of paper, on the
back. The sheet contains the beginning of a letter received by Verlaine, not dated, and in these terms:

> My dear friend, you will not be angry because I seem
> to have neglected you lately? In reality I have been
> working on your behalf, have written to Vanier and
> to Fénéon; I have seen Madame Turquois (? a hardly
> decipherable word). She was expecting your
> mother, but she has probably written to you since,
> and I think . . .

Here the poet cut the paper for his own use. In the
margin at the beginning of the letter addressed to him he
has sketched himself in a large check cape like an English
groom's, with a sort of nightcap pulled well over his
head, and written beside it: "Here I am in my tartan and
'bostron,' in which I flabbergast my colleagues."

I have written to Vanier and to Courtois. . . Verlaine had
been in correspondence with Vanier, his publisher, for
more than a year, but in the two hundred and fifty pages
of letters to him in the second volume of his *Correspondance* there is none dated May 1885. Courtois was a
native of the Ardennes, whom Verlaine had known at
Rethel and whom he had met again in Paris, where he had
set up as a wine-seller in the rue de la Roquette . . .
which was no doubt the reason for Verlaine going to
lodge in the street with the Saturnian name.

The poem on the lost reliquary has been mentioned,

and we observed that it is not, certainly, overflowing
with unction. *Lombes* is a sonnet collected in *Parallèlement:*

Two of the finest women appeared to me that night.

It is dated "Vouziers (Ardennes), April 13th—May
13th, 1885." which covers the whole period of his imprisonment. It would serve vaguely (we have other evidence) to prove that at Coulommes the heresy of the
author of *Hombres* had revived again:

And these women endeavoured to break down the
pride of my desire and were astounded at my
indifference!

The pride of my desire! We know what Verlaine's erotic
Muse meant by that expression as also by this phrase
Bring my pride low! addressed, however, we must hasten
to add, to a woman.

The same volume contains several poems written
after the poet's release which emphasise the metamorphosis of the pseudo-peasant into a quasi-tramp. There
is the poem about the urchins, quoted on page 156, which
is dated "Attigny, May 31st—June 1st, 1885." Then
there is *L'Impudent*, and *L'Impénitent*, which mirrors the
state of mind, and of sexual appetite, of "a worn-out
vagabond with dulled eyes, possessed by an unholy
desire. . ."

Then there is *Guitare* where, under a name evocative
of the cells, the Villonesque name of Pierre Duchâtelet,
"the beggar of the sunken road," sings and speaks.
Obsessed by the memory of Mathilde, the unfortunate
"widower" romances the story of his marriage with the
sentiments and in the language of a real tramp—of the

tramp he has only too truly become. "Should one kill
her or pray for her?" he asks at the end:

> And the Beggar knows very well that he will pray,
> but the Devil would wager that he will kill.

Then follows the *Ballade de la vie en rouge*, the *envoi* of which
calls up the country road with its ruts and the hedge that
served the vagabond for shelter.

During the summer of 1885, with one or two inter-
vals spent in Paris, the poet wandered about the Ardennes
as a tramp—a tramp who did a spot of begging. If this
does not seem credible, read the fragment called *La
Goutte* in his posthumous works. The scene is laid in
that village where the poet "had lived for several years,
spending a not inconsiderable amount of money . . . in
the district that his prodigality, good and bad, had, if
not made wealthy, at least put in easy circumstances"—
a village that we recognise as Coulommes. After two
days stay there, with "visibly empty pockets" and the
refusal of any credit:

> "a poor man whom he had once helped gave him
> shelter for the night in the caravan where he lived
> with his family, a caravan he had made himself from
> odds and ends, and which was dragged about by the
> husband and wife themselves when stone-breaking,
> the osier harvest, the sale of baskets and brushes,
> or the chance of using their little photographer's
> outfit, compelled them to move about. These
> excellent people lent him ten francs; and others as
> good, needy inn-keepers with whom he had spent a
> good deal of cash without keeping much count of
> it, formerly, fifteen francs."

This was easily enough to enable him to get to J . . . .
(that is, Juniville), where a lawyer had some money of
his . . . "but would he let go of it?" The "little town
where he had to take the train," Attigny, was, as ill-luck
would have it, keeping holiday. What with the singing
girls and the games, he passed the night there, and in the
morning found himself with only just enough money for
his ticket. From the station where the train set him
down, "he had to go some five miles on foot, along a
dusty high-road of Champagne, treeless except for a few
sickly bushes." He had three sous left, which he drank,
then he set out on the long trudge. At the same moment,
in Paris, Victor Hugo was being buried, so it was June
1st. It was hot weather for a pedestrian "wearing a top-
hat and a fur-trimmed overcoat," but his hope in the
solicitor lent strength to his legs:

> Half-way there, when I was nearly done in, lo and
> behold, passing through a village I was accosted
> by a beggar I knew. The man said to me: "How
> goes it? It's thirsty weather, will you pay for a
> drink?"
>
> "But I haven't a copper, otherwise, as you know
> very well. . . I'm going on to J . . . . to collect some
> money that's owed me."
>
> "Don't worry about that, I shall be glad if you
> will have one with me, over there, at So and So's.
> Will you?"
>
> "Why, of course."
>
> Facing the church—slate and limestone, like all
> the churches in that part of the country, with a
> broad tower in the centre where one could see the
> bells swinging during the Te deum—is a pleasant

public-house. The Aisne brandy smiled with a
bluish tint through the small, coarse glasses; we
clinked glasses, drank, and by God, it was the best
tot I ever swallowed in my life.

"I'll do the same for you one day, old boy!"

"Oh, nonsense! You're very welcome."

And I, since I it was, went on my way to the
lawyer's (who was away, though, as it turned out),
in livelier mood than Olympio to his Pantheon, at
that same moment.

III.   IN THE SLUMS

How did this cheery vagabondage come to end? What
made his mother consent to live with him again? At what
date did the two of them, cured of the country, return
to the city? Did they come back together or separately?
On October 2nd, 1885, the date when Verlaine gives
Vanier his Paris address, excusing himself for his "immense delay; I have had so many set-backs and bothers,"
was he alone or with her? "I am ill in bed with rheumatism in the joints of my legs." Was it because she knew
him to be ill that the poor old woman forgave him and
hastened to him? The letters to Vanier make no mention
of her being there until December 10th, and then only
in the words: "My mother laid-up in bed." They were
then living behind the Bastille, in the rue Moreau, below
the Vincennes railway, herded among the poor who
crowded this sort of Cour des Miracles, called the Cour
Saint-François. Their place was a furnished one, for the
last of their furniture had been swallowed up in the
Coulommes disaster. But they still had a number of

bonds left, and these they sold one by one to support themselves. It was not to be for long as regards Elisa-Stéphanie-Julie-Josèphe Dehée, the widow Verlaine. On January 21st, 1886, she who in Paradise might claim to have been the most unhappy of all the mothers of poets, even beside the mothers of Villon, of Baudelaire and of Rimbaud, was released from her martyrdom.

Her son did not follow her body to its last resting-place. The rheumatism that was to ensure him the use and enjoyment of the hospitals of the capital confined him to bed, his leg in splints. It was this rheumatism, thanks to which the son was to be enabled to live, that caused the mother's death if we are to believe the *Confessions*:

> She was accustomed to say to me, after our quarrels, "You will see, if you go on like this, I shall go away one day so that you will never know where I am." No, she was not to make good her words, and the proof is that she died from a chill she caught whilst nursing me for the complaint I still suffer from. Ah, I dream of her often, almost always we are quarrelling; I feel that I am in the wrong, I am about to admit it, to implore peace, to fall at her knees filled with such pain for having grieved her, with such affection for her evermore, all devotion to her. . . She has disappeared! And the rest of my dream fades out in the increasing anguish of an endless, useless search. . . But no! She lives, my mother lives in my soul, and I swear to her here that her son lives with her, weeps in her bosom, suffers for her, and was never for one instant, even in his worst errors, weaknesses rather! without feeling himself

under her protection, her reproaches and continual loving encouragement! . . .

And he did not even see her die, for, as Delahaye tells us, her room was on the first floor and Verlaine's on the ground-floor:

> "Paralysed, unable to move with his leg in the splints, he wished to be carried upstairs to the dying woman; but the staircase was not wide enough to allow a stretcher to pass."

Was this the ground-floor room or was it a different one (in any case it was in the Cour Saint-François) where Lepelletier came to see him, informed by a letter of January 26th of his bereavement, his illness and his address?

> Verlaine was lodging with the keeper of a wine-shop. . . One had to go through the open bar to reach the poet's room . . . small, sordid, and sinister as the cut-throat alley at the end of which it was hidden.
>
> There were no floor-boards, not even tiles. One trod on bare earth. It was slightly muddy. The wet brought in from outside by the customers soaked into this far from urban soil. The wine-seller's boy, who brought him his scanty rations, infrequent friends from the Latin Quarter who came to have a drink at the bar so close to the sick man's bed, and an obliging neighbour who used to talk to the poet in the evening, lend him papers, and perform small nursing duties, these were his only visitors.
>
> A tiny cupboard served as a bookcase. He had

crammed into it what few books he had saved from
his numerous wrecks and some manuscripts.   A
narrow table and two straw-bottomed chairs. . .

One begins to understand, after that, how Verlaine,
who had not thought himself too badly off in prison, was
to consider himself well off in a hospital. Knowing, too,
that the complaint that sent him there was not dangerous,
that in ten years it was only to make him "a sort of healthy
invalid," we can understand the "frank admission" he
made in 1885, having already practised it a good deal,
the sort of declaration of affection contained in *Bonheur*
for

> this sort of convent, though lacking the Christian
> hope. The world is such that I want for nothing
> and I would be willing to stay here all my life;

and the apostrophe with which, in 1891, he wound up
Mes Hôpitaux:

> So, then, my hospitals of these last years, *adieu!* . . .
> unless it is to be *Au revoir*, but, in any case, Hail! I
> have lived peacefully and industriously under your
> roofs and I have not left you one by one without
> being sorry in some way; and if my dignity as a man
> relatively less, but not greatly less, wretched than
> the most penniless of those who frequent you, and
> my right instincts as a good citizen who does not
> wish to usurp the place so much desired by so
> many poor folk, often forced me, prematurely often,
> to leave your gates, so blessed on arrival but not
> more than on going away; you may be certain, good

hospitals, that in spite of the inevitable monotony
and a necessarily strict discipline and inconveniences
inherent in any human situation, I retain a memory
of you that is unique among so many other memories
infinitely more painful that the outside life has
made me, still makes me and will make me, without
any doubt, suffer again and always.

Verlaine still gave that hovel as his "town address" on
December 13th, 1886, writing to Lepelletier.   But in
February, though, as we learn from a letter to Vanier of
the 6th, he was offered a bed in a hospital.   "It is a little
too traditional, too poetic, perhaps, that, the Hospital.
However tempting it may be, I shall wait a bit yet."
Besides, this offer was conditional on a recommendation,
and an efficacious one was not to be found at a moment's
notice.   It was not until July that he succeeded, and as a
result he passed that month and the two following at
the Tenon hospital, "having sores on the legs."   When he
wrote to Lepelletier, on December 13th, he had been
nursed for the past six weeks at the Broussais hospital
because of anchylosis of the left knee resulting from the
hydarthrosis of the previous winter.

Then, what had he lived on until that July and afterwards during the short interval between his leaving the
Tenon and entering the Broussais?   In the first place, on
money realised by the sale of his last bonds, on those
which the judge had left to him, in agreement with the
claimants, out of the bundle which had been distrained
on when his mother's room had been sealed up after her
death.   Following this agreement, the judge had declared
that "he had acted like an honest man."

One of his letters, which I have not been able to find

among the confusion of his correspondence, shows that he was proud of having earned this testimonial. Another (to Lepelletier, 21st October, 1887) argues that Society having, after all, robbed him, in the person of the judge of the XII arrondissement, "owes him," perhaps, a little hospitality. On May 10th previously, in a letter to Vanier, an idea had struck him:

> An idea: I surrendered my bonds to my wife, *then not yet re-married, and for the child.* Now she refuses me everything as regards the child, sight and news of him and his education, and, I am told, has him brought up with the children (for it seems that he has some, too) of her "husband." Now I find myself, all debts settled, in absolute destitution, and it occurs to me to appeal to the judge who authorised the seizure and who congratulated me on my upright behaviour in this matter, so that he, a judge and with all the facts before him, should induce Madame? to do her little bit of duty and allow me a few sous out of the twenty thousand francs and more she had from me voluntarily. Don't you think so?

Voluntarily . . . ? We must not enquire too closely whether, if his leg had not been in splints, it would not have turned out to be with a very bad grace. We shall find him several times regretting the intervention of the judge and complaining, in verse, of being lodged in a hospital "through the act of a thieving woman" (*Bonheur*, Poem x, dated 1888); or, in prose, declaring himself in a letter to Vanier, November 9th, 1887, "at bottom, a very honourable man, reduced to poverty through an

excess of delicacy and good-nature, but at every point a
gentleman and a hidalgo."

But twenty-thousand francs, not to mention the *and
more!* the figure is really much too high. It would mean
that when his mother died she left double that sum; as
it seems likely that the agreement authorised by the
judge cut the apple—I should say the bundle of bonds—
in half. But a letter to Vanier of 26th January fixes the
amount he inherited from his mother at three thousand
five hundred francs, "after all deductions consequent on
my wife's claim of January 25th, 1886"—a sum from
which nearly three thousand francs had to be deducted
for the expenses of her last illness and the funeral. But
it is possible that the smaller figure is no more correct
than the larger one.

His bonds, or what remained of them, were held for
him by his landlord, old Chanzy, who did not neglect to
subtract what was owing to him or what he claimed
to be. This gave rise to a "Chanzy case," mentioned in
the letter to Vanier of December 9th, 1886:

> I shall not return to the Chanzy business except to
> tell you that that robber ought to send you some
> bills of mine, and I believe, God help me, a good
> deal of money, a great deal of money he owes me, a
> great deal; so, you will bring it or send it to me as
> quickly as possible, won't you?

He also had the legacy bequeathed him by his aunt
Rose, his mother's sister, who had died in February. This
he estimated at the equivalent of two thousand four
hundred francs in cash (in a letter to Lepelletier of 13th
December). On 26th January, 1887, when it had long
been spent, he told Vanier:

"From my aunt's legacy, which I had to legally abandon to escape a fresh distraint, property worth fifteen hundred francs and railway shares (I think) seven or eight hundred."

IV. HOSPITALS AND FURNISHED ROOMS

Between the death of his mother and his entering the Tenon Hospital, Pauvre Lélian, apart from these bequests, lived on what he could draw from Vanier, who published *Jadis et Naguère* and *Les Poètes maudits* in 1884, *Mémoires d'un Veuf* and *Louise Leclercq* in 1886; he was also waiting to publish *Amour*, the manuscript of which he was not given till 1887. Verlaine also received advances for the notices he wrote for the series *Hommes d'aujourd'hui*. But Vanier sold these *Hommes* at ten centimes each, and his editions consisted of only six hundred copies (in the case of the *Poètes maudits*, of only two hundred and fifty three), priced at three francs, which was unusually high. This was a period when the public did not buy books, because they cost nothing. In 1886 Vanier bought up the first edition of *Sagesse*, or rather the few copies of it that remained mouldering in the cellars of Palmé, the publishers. So we shall not be surprised if at that time he rarely paid out more than twenty francs at a time, and if the average was a five-franc piece. Among Verlaine's innumerable letters to Vanier there are not a dozen that are not dictated by a need of money as imperious, as urgent—as necessity itself. "I, who am always bothering you, but am even more bothered myself . . ."—this opening of a note of February 24th,

1887, could serve as a pattern, if we may say so, of the whole correspondence.

And there would be no more heart-breaking example of the relations between poet and publisher if Verlaine had been capable of unhappiness at that time. He was less capable of it than ever and his declaration in the *Confessions*: "I have never been melancholy in my life," is supported by his letters. The Verlaine of those last years was as unfortunate as could be, but he was the reverse of miserable. He owes this to his natural propensity and to a long acclimatisation to misfortune, but it was also an advantage he derived from literature; right up to the end he was to be as happy as a child with his writings, done at leisure and bringing him in money. See how he exclaims at the very moment (1st October, 1886), when the Cour Saint-François had him in its grip:

> My dear Vanier, I am filled with jubilation. Found masses of things, prose and verse, I had thought lost. Seen Izambard, who has lent me early poems by Rimbaud. Plan definitely fixed for *Madame Aubin*, which will be in one act only. In labour with two long chapters for *Mémoires d'un Veuf*. Have written verses for serious, paying Reviews (Prudence and Chastity), which do pay. Some very daring biographical verses are just going to be published by *Lutèce*. Hang it! I'm burning my boats. Chatter and publicity.
>
> Did you see, in the *France* of about a week ago, a laudatory quotation by Marcel Fouquier?

So there is no need to be more royalist than the king, and we may unravel, without emotion, from his letters to

Lepelletier and Vanier, the list of his various lodgings and his financial conditions.

As for the "verses for serious Reviews," this must refer to Poem XII in *Bonheur*, where following this heroic stanza:

> Warlike, soldierly and virile at every point, holy Chastity that God sees the first of all the virtues marching in His radiance, only the least distance behind Charity,

Chastity receives a rather ludicrous homage, as singular as the obsession (already pointed out) of this satyr, in his singing moments at least, with that theological virtue. Can one imagine Lamartine or Sully-Prudhomme chanting the praises of lust?

In December 1886 he was, as we saw, in the Broussais Hospital; he spent the following January and February there, and in March moved to the Cochin Hospital, all the time "in the most absolute poverty" (to Lepelletier, on the 10th). On May 23rd, he was in the *Asile National* at Vincennes. "I am writing to you," he tells Vanier, "pressed by the most absolute and real need." He remained there till Friday, July 1st, on which day, as he told Vanier three days before, he was "obliged to leave in order to come back in a few days time. It is compulsory, a nuisance, but compulsory." On July 15th: "I got into the Tenon with the greatest of ease," but, "reduced to sevenpence"; therefore, quickly,

> "another little advance of five francs on our agreements. . . All the same it is piteous to live like this! I assure you I could weep for it. But I will do nothing that is not dignified and simple. *Potius*

mori quam foedari; that is truly my motto. And to die a Christian death, worthy of my parents and an example to my son. . . Yours very cordially, and very sadly, but determined to be firm."

On August 7th he was still at the Tenon, but this time writes to Lepelletier: "*Not a penny.* The little money Vanier still owes me can't amount to more than a few five-franc pieces." He has ·only to wait "till November 15th next, for nine hundred francs from a solicitor who is adamant against any advance whatever." In the meantime he gets advances on contributions to the papers, thinks that he might give English lessons, "but to whom and where?" and cherishes the distant hope of a grant from the Ministry of Education.

On August 9th he was in the *Asile National* at Vincennes, as he informs Vanier—in the Argand Ward, room 8, bed 13. Public admitted from 12 till 4 on Thursdays and Sundays. "The five-franc piece very nearly exhausted and I need those dark grey trousers, about three francs." On September 9th he was obliged to leave this refuge and to embark on manœuvres which came to a successful end on the 20th, when he again found shelter in the Broussais.

26th September, 1887, Salle Follin, Bed 22. My dear friend, received here like the prodigal son. Mild reproaches at the most. And arrived here in very good style, in spite of all the absinthes. Must confess that before setting out, and after having settled for my lodgings, I had a very excellent feed which, by the way, took the shine off my last rescue medal.

It is true that he "made a blunder in not spending more judiciously" the money from his publisher and Coppée's fifty francs. But why had not the latter sent them to him direct with a note, or, handed them to him?

I really do think I should have made better use of them and not have found myself obliged to make a meal off two rolls and some bitters, at times!

But never fear he has "had his fling" and clearly realises "his very gloomy position."

Well, time will tell ! . . . In the meanwhile, I am going to get twenty-five francs for a contribution to a Review. I shall carefully put twenty francs aside, so that when I have to leave here in the early morning, I can get myself a room for a fortnight. . . But I shall also have to have something to eat at home, costing twenty francs a fortnight. . . And then my credit at Juniville falls due, I shall be getting my nine hundred and forty francs. The moral is, for you to help me, and so let me know the best you can do.

Poverty, Infirmity, Hope. That is his motto in a letter to Lepelletier, on the 27th. And hope supports him through an attack of depression indicated in a letter to Vanier at the end of November: "I am mortally fed up, truly! Because of this endless seclusion I see my hopes fading. So long, obviously, as I am in this prison, this sepulchre. . ."

This attack was not unconnected with the miscarrying of that remittance of nine hundred and forty francs. But he is determined to bestir himself, to convince himself, to prove that he is neither dead nor dying "nor renounc-

M

ing anything at all either of my rights as a man or a
writer." His calculations establish to a certainty that
he can put up a fight. He is not going to fail!

He was still at the Broussais on January 3rd, 1888.
The solicitor's nine hundred francs will come for certain
in April or May, for as he had told Vanier the November
before, "I had made a mistake as to the immediate realis-
ability of what is due to me at Juniville. It is due in
April, the solicitor says, and *solicitors are never mistaken,*"
and he wrote the last words in enormous capitals. From
what other Bohemian has the honourable corporation of
solicitors ever received such a mark of confidence? But
Verlaine, for all his sincerity, uses this Juniville debt to
extract small sums from Vanier, which were covered
already by the purchase, for two hundred and fifty
francs, of a new edition of *Poèmes saturniens* and *La Bonne
Chanson.* On the 3rd January, however, he says that in the
interval till April or May, Vanier will not be able to let
him have more than two hundred or two hundred and
fifty francs. His leg is not going on badly, his general
health is good; at this "peaceful Broussais" he can work
in quiet and "*Amour* will be published very soon."

On March 10th letters to Vanier and Leo d'Orfer, the
editor of *Lutèce*, show that he was still in the Broussais.
In a later letter to d'Orfer, on the 21st, he gives his
address at 14 rue Royer-Collard. This is the first private
address his letters give, I believe, since his leaving the
Cour Saint-François in April 1887. This commences
that succession of furnished rooms in the Latin Quarter,
the last of which, 39 rue Descartes, was to give up its
tenant on January 8th, 1896; rather on the 10th, for
Verlaine's funeral took place two days after his death.

A letter to an unknown correspondent, September

29th, gives this same address and this rue Royer-Collard whose name, so symbolical of the conventions and of respectability, recalls a passage in *Romances sans paroles:*

> Some well-dressed gentlemen, no doubt friends of the Royer-Collards, are going up to the mansion. I should think it fine to be those old men!

But at the end of November (letter to Vanier) he was lodging at 216 rue Saint-Jacques; but he did not stay there long. We find him installed in the Broussais about December 20th (letter to Savine), and there he remained till April. In May he was at 4 rue de Vaugirard, and it does not seem that he went into hospital again till February, 1889, and then it was the Broussais once more. So he went for nearly a year without needing a hospital. This phenomenon is explained by the arrival of the nine hundred francs from the solicitor, the repayment of about a thousand francs owing to his mother from a native of Arras, some contributions to the papers, and Vanier's advances on *Parallèlement* and the new edition of *Sagesse.* (Note 20.)

Perhaps also by the repayment of a sum from a personal debtor, a certain Abbé Salard: "I shall make plans, as soon as I get my thousand francs from my solicitor, to recover a little later—from a one-time curate at Saint-Gervais—a sum of fifteen hundred francs. (A hard nut, a curate of Saint-Gervais but it's a nice morsel, fifteen hundred francs)," he wrote to Lepelletier on October 21st, 1887.

On September 20th, 1884, he had received from the archbishopric of Paris this letter:

> Sir, I have the honour to inform you that M. l'Abbé Salard has had no duties in the diocese since January

1884, nor, I believe, has he been living in it. From enquiries made, it appears that he lived in Paris for some time, Cité Trevise, 7, and also at the presbytery of Courute (Mayenne).

It was perhaps with this refractory debtor in mind that our creditor wrote Poem xi of *Bonheur*:

Priests of Jesus Christ, the Truth preserves you! Ah, though you be what I think a chattering crowd, or what the thinker, himself, says of you: Meanly ambitious, spitefully jealous, grasping, impure, hard-hearted, the Truth preserves you!

The Truth looks after the priests as the Law does the solicitors.

IN RETIREMENT

On June 21st, 1889, his household gods returned to 4 rue Vaugirard, the Hotel de Lisbonne. It was here, during the last year but one of his life, that his good samaritan and perfect portraitist, F. A. Cazals, looked after him for a long period. August 2nd, he wrote from the Broussais to Lepelletier. On August 11th to *"Monsieur* Vanier" (with whom I am very distant, and for a good reason," he told Lepelletier):

> I wish to put my affairs in order and I have been looking over the agreements signed between us. I require to know if all the undertakings you have given me have been fulfilled:
>
> 1. Is the edition of *Mémoires d'un Veuf* sold out, or how many copies have you left?
>
> 2. You have reprinted the *Fêtes galantes* and the *Romances sans paroles* in editions of six hundred of each work. Are these sold out, or how many copies remain?
>
> The same enquiries for *les Poètes maudits*, *Amour Parallèlement*, *Jadis et Naguère*, *Sagesse*, *Poèmes saturniens:*
>
> I await your reply or your visit. With compliments. . .

But let us cut short at this point the record of a poverty which is no longer agonising and has had from this date

183

many exact historians. Food and lodging, and more besides, were never to be wanting again to this—what shall we call him?—established Bohemian. In September he was well enough off to go to Aix-les-Bains to be treated for his rheumatism. Among his admirers there were several who were liberal. Without losing Vanier's small instalments he found in Léon Deschamps, proprietor of *La Plume*, a financial backer and organiser of assistance, whose zeal and disinterestedness will be appreciated by those who have examined the relative documents, taking into account the limited resources of *La Plume* and of its proprietor, and also the little disposition the poet had to economy. I notice in a letter from Deschamps to René Ghil discussing the publication by subscription of *Dédicaces* in 1890:

> "For a single book published by *La Plume*, Verlaine draws more than he did from all his past works. He has been on a frightful binge, the author of *Sagesse*. I have given him six hundred francs in one week. He got through it all. I am going to put the brake on."

Six hundred francs in one week! Oh, Royer-Collard! In 1890 a student who received two hundred and fifty francs a month from his family was considered well-off. But, without mentioning casual pick-ups, had not Verlaine two mistresses to look after in Philomène Boudin called Esther, and Eugénie Krantz: the first when he was very hard up, the second when he was less so; the second was not a bad sort, and to her he owed a home during the last year or so of his life, and one which seemed almost conjugal when he died. A home! In 1890 Verlaine had not yet contemplated that solution, it required rather larger resources than he had then; but for one who had been the beggar of Coulommes and the tenant of a hovel in the Cour Moreau, it was comforting to know that when his purse was empty or his leg rebelled against excess of absinthe or love-making, thirty sous (the price of a cab in those days), was all that was needed to get one into hospital. To get into hospital, be received with open arms, to find clean sheets, warmth, something to eat and writing materials, not to mention the medical attention; to receive all the visitors one liked, who ranged from Comte Robert de Montesquiou to Bibi la Purée and included all the young writers and painters of the advance guard who counted. And what could be more jolly than the life of the Latin Quarter, when one had been put on one's feet by the doctors and nurses; when one could return to eat, drink, argue about æsthetics at the Café François-Premier, the Luxembourg, and pass the evenings at the Soleil d'Or, limp about and make love till one's pockets were empty or till one's stiff leg became impossible to move!   (Note 21.)

Pauvre Lélian had a greater thirst for social intercourse than ever, and he had never enjoyed it so widely and so tranquilly. So tranquilly, so assured about the future that he lost his faith and (passato il pericolo, gabato il santo!) and states the fact without regret:

I was a mystic and am so no longer, Woman has completely dominated me again,

for even if one is the least vain of great poets (after the incredible Ponchon), how could one not relish a renown so flattering as that which was now Verlaine's? The article by Jules Lemaître in the Revue bleue on January 7th, 1888, had been influential, and in 1891 his Choix de

Poèmes, published now by a commercial publisher, began
to bring him a monetary equivalent to his fame.

> Received of MM. Charpentier and Fasquelle, on
> account of author's royalties, errors and omissions
> excepted, the seventh, eighth, ninth and tenth
> thousand copies, one thousand, nine hundred
> francs, payment made April 11th, 1896,

as we read in the accounts of the settlement of his estate.

This volume contained his portrait as conceived by
the least objective of portraitists; and the legend of the
"tender Verlaine" received such an impetus from it that
the poet himself was taken in, and even came at times to
look like this bold idealisation. But to know what his
appearance really was, one must study the portraits by
Cazals, rather than that one by Carrière.

His sayings and doings were recorded by the gossip-
writers; the least literary of the periodicals were ready
to take the slightest fragment from his pen, though unfortunately he produced little now. Vanier still published,
at six hundred copies, it is true, the thin volumes that
profane love inspired, as well as his prose: *Mes Hôpitaux*,
1891, *Mes Prisons* 1893; and it was not the fault of the
Fin de Siècle if he ceased to give them more instalments of
his *Confessions*, the beginning of which, published in
volume form by that periodical, sold like hot cakes.

His autograph manuscripts, which he used to prepare
in hospital when no visiting was allowed, sold for not
less than a franc a line, at least if they were not longer
than a sonnet. Holland, in November 1892, Belgium,
in February and March 1893, his beloved England, in
November 1893, welcomed him as a lecturer and did not

send him back with an empty purse. He lectured besides
at Nancy.

All this did not enrich him for long, especially if we
include the famous performance of his play *Les Uns et les
Autres* at the Vaudeville, which, he said, had been got up
for his discomfiture, not his benefit; but it kept him
going. It kept him going, thanks to the devotion—one
must call things by their proper names—of Eugénie
Krantz, who had become decidedly his "real wife" and
who helped with the household expenses by making
shirts for the Belle Jardinière. He would go out on the
spree (and others with him, as we have seen, without his
permission), and she lets him off with one of those
"scoldings" which *Odes en son honneur* are not silent about.
For Eugénie is not Mathilde, for a little punishment does
not come amiss when one is in love, and when one re-
turns it, and it is a nurse almost as much as a woman that
he needs. He has a good time, and one fine day he even
had enough on him to be robbed, which was a lesson to
him for having renewed relations with Philomène, since
her husband was to be strongly suspected. But hang it!
A wound in the purse is not fatal, "Seriously, I am working, and seriously I count on recovering from the mis-
adventure of the thousand francs" (letter to Vanier, 27th
December, 1892). The first grant from the Ministry—
everything comes to those who can wait—arrived soon
afterwards, reducing the extent of the calamity by half.

He was proclaimed Prince of Poets on the death of
Leconte de Lisle, and his project, announced in 1894, of
standing for the Academy, was less facetious than might
be thought, but first of all he had to obtain his re-
admission to the Hôtel de Ville, and he began to think of
this again. A Bohemian in retirement, he did not pursue

respectability with less vigour than his two Sultanas, and what a great step it was in that direction to have lectured at Brussels before an audience of lawyers in that same law-court where, twenty years before. . . Certainly, those days are a long way off, when:

The bourgeois persecution killed his good name!

That is one reason why the social order, patriotism and the family will find nothing to complain of in what he writes. To say that this victim of Saturn was to finish by spending more happy moments than painful ones would not be extravagant, perhaps.

But the furnished room, spotlessly kept, as I can testify like all those who saw him there in his last sleep, the "home" in which Eugénie Krantz with her sewing machine, and he with his plans, spent the winter of 1895-6, was not, all the same, warm. A cold on the lungs is soon caught. The one which attacked him at the beginning of January did not delay so long as his leg had done.

APPENDICES

NOTES

Note 1 Page 40

The present volume was finished before the appearance, at the end of 1928, of that interesting work by M. Le Febve de Vivy (Miette, Brussels), *Les Verlaines*. We learn from this that the poet's paternal ancestors were not so completely reliable as I had imagined. In particular, his grandfather, the solicitor, born in 1769; he was a wily and quarrelsome man who divided his time between church and drink, till he became a militant atheist without ceasing to be a drunkard. "With his occasional outbursts of extravagant, but simple-minded folly, the grandfather was the anticipation of the grandson," the historian records.

Among other information regarding the early development of Verlaine's alcoholism and his horrible treatment of his mother we may consult a letter dated "Batignolles, 18th July, 1869." It was written to M. Pérot, burgomaster of Paliseul and a close relation of the Verlaines, by a young servant girl of that town who had been in the service of Mde. Grandjean, the poet's paternal aunt, and had been kept on for some time after her sister-in-law's death by Mde. Verlaine.

Note 2 Page 40

Enlisted in the 5th Battery of Sappers, June 20th, 1814. Transferred to the 2nd Engineer Regiment until September 30th, 1816. Corporal in the 1st Engineers, October 1st, 1816. Fourrier on October 27th, 1817. Sergeant on August 1st, 1819. Sergeant-major on February 23rd, 1824. Second Lieutenant on June 30th, 1828. First Lieutenant on 30th September of the same year. Junior Captain on December 27th, 1833. Transferred to the 3rd Engineers as Senior Captain, January 10th, 1844. Retired on March 31st, 1848.

April 7th-December 30th, 1823, with the 2nd Corps of the Army of Spain, then returned to France. From 1825-1828 attached to the Army of Occupation of Cadiz. 11th May, 1830-11th January, 1831 to the Army of Africa.

Chevalier of the First Class in the Royal and Military Order of Ferdinand of Spain on 12th March, 1829. Chevalier of the Legion of Honour 27th December, 1830.

191

Note 3 Page 42

The quotations from Edmond Lepelletier are taken from his *Paul Verlaine, sa vie, son œuvre.* (Published by the Société du Mercure de France in 1907.)

Those from Ernest Delahaye, with Lepelletier the only original first-hand biographer of the poet (for his whole life, at least, for his later years have not lacked historians), are from his *Verlaine.* (Messein, 1919.)

Note 4 Page 59

The portraits of Verlaine's father and mother are reproduced in the *Verlaine* of MM. Alph. Séché and J. Bertaut (Michaud, 1912). This volume is invaluable for its illustrations and gives as well the portrait of Verlaine as a child referred to on page 60. It contains besides portraits of Rimbaud, Lucien Létinois and others who played a part in the poet's life, numerous drawings by M. F-A. Cazals, the excellent portraitist of his later years.

Note 5 Page 62

The poem imitated by Verlaine has the title of *Reverie*, and not *Mignon.* Here are two stanzas of it, the first and the last, corresponding to those we gave of *Marco:*

When Mignon went by the excited bees flew to brush her ruddy lips and the ears of corn and the wild-roses bent to kiss her fingers. The whole world was love and reverie. The stream gliding in its silver bed pursued her, and the wind caressed the grass that her feet had hardly bowed, when Mignon passed by.

But when she loved, when the beautiful Mignon had chosen the friend, the heart worthy of her! What a golden dream! What heavenly rejoicings!

It was an unending honeymoon! . . . He has not touched her lips of fire; man is not made for such kisses as those. He looked in her eyes and saw the heaven he dreamed of. And touching her hand, he breathed his last, he whom Mignon loved.

Note 6 Page 63

"Not virtuous, evidently, but not vicious either."

As the reader will no doubt agree (unless sharing our parents' masculinist prejudice about courtesans), if I transcribe the first verse of Marco's song, which the acquaintances of Verlaine in his later years heard him humming more than once:

Marco the beautiful, what do you love? Is it the joyful music
to which the dancers sway in the flower-decked ballroom?
Is it the trembling murmur of the poplars in the dusk of night
whispering with the breeze?
No! no! no! no!
Then Marco, what do you love?
Not the song of the linnet? Not the voice of the stream? Not
the cry of the lark? Nor the voice of Romeo?
(*Jingling of golden coins.*)
No! that is what Marco loves.

Note 7 Page 67

In the author's *Problème de Rimbaud*, and especially in his *La Vie
de Rimbaud et de son Œuvre* (Mercure de France, 1929), will be found
an analysis of Verlaine's erotic psychology (as well as of that of
Rimbaud), which does not cover the same ground as the one given
in the present volume.

Note 8 Page 87

The *Mémoires* of Mathilde Mauté are still in manuscript; the
portions quoted were disclosed by M. Georges Maurevert in the
Eclaireur de Nice for 26th December, 1913, with the title *Mémoires
de Celle qui fut Madame Paul Verlaine*. In *Figaro* for May 31st, 1912,
M. Fernand Vanderem gave an account of an interview with the
poet's ex-wife; he reproduced in a life-like way the account she
gave him of the departure of Verlaine with Rimbaud and of her own
journey to Brussels.

I wrote to him and finally obtained his consent to see me in
Brussels. I went with my mother, leaving the child in Paris.
I met Verlaine. It was in the morning, in a small hotel, the
Hôtel Liégeois, I believe. I begged him to come back to
Paris. He refuses. I suggest that we should travel. He refuses.
Then an idea came to me. Suppose we should go to Canada?
Yes, over there were old friends of his from the days of the
Commune, Louise Michel amongst others. We should have
connections. There would be the change of scene. This
seemed to attract him. He asked to have until the evening to
consider it.

In the evening, at five o'clock, I met him in a public garden
near the station. He had a rather morose expression, as he
often had after he had been to the café. And immediately he
told me vaguely that he would agree. I turn towards my
mother: "What does he say?" "He agrees." "To what?" "I

N

haven't grasped exactly, but let us take advantage of his wanting to come. We shall see afterwards."

We get to the station, enter the Paris train. We eat some cold chicken. Verlaine does not say a word, but pulls his hat over his eyes and goes to sleep. We get out for the Customs. When that is over there is no Verlaine. We look about and call him. No one. The porters make us get in. I was distracted. Suddenly, on the platform, right in front of us, whom do we see? It is Verlaine who is looking at us with a fixed expression. "Get in quickly, the train is going," mother called to him. Verlaine still stares at us with that fixed expression, and says "I am staying!" And he crammed his soft hat on his head with a great gesture.

And that is all, Sir; I never saw him afterwards. . .

Note 9 Page 88

This is a thing which Lepelletier emphasises, but the study of the marriage-contract drawn up the 23rd-24th June, 1870, before Maître Taupin at Clichy, does not prove that Mathilde made such a very advantageous marriage.

Verlaine contributed forty-seven thousand francs of which twenty thousand francs were advanced him by his mother on his inheritance, and she retained the right to receive this sum back if Verlaine died without children.

Mathilde contributed a sum of four thousand two hundred francs; furniture and linen to the value of five thousand seven hundred and ninety-four francs; jewellery and wedding presents valued at twelve hundred francs; and Government 3 per cent. stock, fifty francs.

Note 10 Page 88

Here is a specimen of Mathilde's poetry:

How powerful is a woman's tear!
A signal to the feeling heart
That takes the lovely, weak one's part,
Of danger drawing near.

A dreadful weapon 'twixt the lids
Of an indomitable She,
That gives deep wounds, as you will see,
Unless you do all that she bids.

Just to begin with, angry looks;
But this is nothing but a skirmish;

'Neath frowning brows her clear eyes tarnish
With anger and gleam sharp as hooks.

Then bitter tears rain from her eyes,
True tears of mystery are these,
Soon swelling into floods and seas
Broken with sobs and storms of sighs.

But to dry up these brackish springs
Ask pardon as she understands,
By pouring in her dimpled hands
Jewels, ribbons, flowers and pretty things.

And this is doubly regrettable, for when the little girl in "the grey
and green tucked dress" perpetrated it, she had no suspicion that
her own eyes were so soon to have cause to weep.

Note 11 Page 88

For an account of the Verlaine household and Rimbaud's intru-
sion see the chapter entitled "Le Divorce de Verlaine" in the
author's *Au Cœur de Verlaine et de Rimbaud*, as well as his *Problème de
Rimbaud* and particularly his *Vie de Rimbaud et de son œuvre*.

Note 12 Page 90

In *La Connaissance* for November 1920, M. Pierre Dufay published a letter and some notes of Verlaine, hitherto unknown.

The letter must be dated the end of 1869 or beginning of 1870
and runs:

A thousand thanks for your kind thought. Probably at any
other time I should have yielded to the temptation of getting
on such an influential paper as the *Gaulois*. But really at the
present moment (and especially as I have a whole heap of
literary plans on hand) I cannot collaborate, *Republican that I
am*, in a thing that, from what the person who came to see me
this morning told me, will be nothing less than "agreeable"
and against the "Mandat impérative."

Note 13 Page 94

Mathilde Mauté's petition for a separation remained unpublished
except for some fragments given in the author's *Au Cœur de Verlaine et de Rimbaud*, till published by him in the *Mercure de France*
for February 15th, 1927. And here is the judgment given by the
Tribunal de la Seine, April 24th, 1874:

The marriage between the Demoiselle Mauté and the Sieur Verlaine having taken place in August, 1870, and seeing that shortly after his marriage, Verlaine fell into the habit of drinking and getting drunk; and that in that condition he frequently committed serious violence against his wife; that he admitted to this violence and these habits in a letter he wrote to his wife on January 20th, 1872; and as it is shown by Verlaine's correspondence, that he abandoned the conjugal domicile to go and live in Brussels, where he gave way without restraint to his habit of drunkenness; that this correspondence further establishes the fact that Verlaine had immoral relations with a young man; that he was sentenced on August 8th, 1873, by the Criminal Court of Brussels, to two years imprisonment and a fine of two hundred francs for assaulting and wounding this person, a violence he committed in a fit of jealousy. . . these facts constituting serious outrage and ill-usage of a kind to procure the judicial separation requested by the wife of Verlaine. For these reasons it is declared that the marriage is dissolved and that the mother is to have the custody of the child.

The liquidation of the conjugal estate shall be proceeded with . . . Order Verlaine to pay his wife alimony of one hundred francs a month quarterly in advance from the date of the petition for a separation till the completion of the liquidation and to pay costs. . .

Note 14 Page 100

Compare in *Laeti et errabundi:*

We had left all impediments behind in Paris, without regret: he some flouted fools and I a certain Princess Souris, a stupid fool. . .

Note 15 Page 116

In a new revue published in the Ardennes, *La Grive* (No. 2, January, 1929), M. O. Guelliot published a letter Verlaine wrote from Rethel on October 27th, 1878, to Sivry It gaily mingles literature, music and drawing with "the things of religion" and gives, as early as that, the text of a Catholic poem which the poet was to wait till 1892 before publishing—in *Liturgies intimes* and which may claim to be one of the least mediocre of the poems in that mediocre volume.

Note 16 Page 129

In April 1924 the *Excelsior* gave a summary of a communication from an old pupil of Verlaine's at Rethel. . . "He was besides, an excellent teacher, at least in the mornings. For indeed, incorrigible as he was, the gentle Lélian got into the habit of going down into the town, after the morning classes at 10.30 to a small bar, *Au Père Martin*. And there he imbibed so many absinthes that he was often incapable of getting back to the school without assistance. It need hardly be said that on those days he could not take his afternoon classes. So the headmaster was soon obliged to give him only classes in the mornings, and was glad to be finally rid of him in July, 1879."

Note 17 Page 130

Besides the information gathered by us verbally about Verlaine's visit to England with Lucien in 1879, we possess a written document of the date, February 20th, 1890. It was written from Coulommes to a native of the Ardennes who had settled in Paris and it was he who furnished us with this letter and explained the circumstances by which he came to receive it:

At the time when Verlaine came to settle in the Attigny district I was about twelve years old. It was not long before the new comer made himself the principal subject of local scandal and I remember the sneering smile with which my parents used to speak of "the Coulommes Englishman," of that s . . . (here an unwritable word), Verlaine. Nobody knew anything about the past life of this singular character nor suspected that he was a poet.

My friend learnt this in 1885, and some time later wrote to a Coulommes friend for information.

This friend who supplied the information died about ten years ago when over the age of seventy. He was for a long time a schoolmaster at Coulommes, and he settled in the village on his retirement. He has always been spoken of to me as a perfectly honourable man, as intelligent, prudent and scrupulous a witness as one could wish. His testimony seems to me, taken on its own merits, to deserve all confidence. He relates several facts which, though common property now, in 1890 and for years afterwards were unknown outside the district. For instance, Verlaine's imprisonment at Vouziers. I consider it the best existing document for that period of the poet's life which still remains so obscure. Here is the part relating to the stay in England:

My dear —, I shall be delighted to tell you what I know of Paul Verlaine and his stay at Coulommes. . .

In 1887 or 8 a young man from Coulommes, Lucien Létinois, was a boarder at the school of Notre-Dame at Rethel where M.

Verlaine taught history, geography and English. Lucien was charming, gay and very playful. M. Verlaine became so attached to him that one day we heard in Coulommes that Lucien, who had just failed in his leaving examination, would not return home for the holidays nor return to the school next term, but was leaving for England with one of his masters.

What they did there I can't really recall, though I have talked to them several times about their stay there.

Did they visit the country as tourists, like the happy pair they were? Or did M. Verlaine give French lessons in some wealthy house? Both hypotheses are admissible. Their stay in England lasted from the beginning of August till the following January. At that date one heard that Lucien had returned home with his friend.

Some time after their arrival Lucien came to see me and suggested that I should make the acquaintance of M. Verlaine, which I agreed to eagerly. I did not know then, however, that M. Verlaine was a poet and even an author of some renown. They came to see me the same evening and came back again several times. We talked about the school at Rethel where I had had the honour (?) to be an assistant master. We talked about England, about the English language, of which I had some knowledge, about politics, journalism and literature. I enjoyed my conversations with this gentleman. His delivery was colourless, his gestures restrained; without being witty his conversation was very interesting.

He was about forty at the time. At Rethel he had said that he was a bachelor and he was believed to be so at Coulommes. It was not until later, at the time of his second stay at Coulommes that it was learnt that he was married and had a son. One of his last books of poems, of which he sent me a copy some two years ago, has this dedication: To my son, Georges Verlaine.

This warm friendship between a man of forty and a young man of eighteen was, as you can imagine, the subject of much discussion. There was certainly something abnormal about it. The two friends were openly accused of sodomy, and Verlaine's undisguised dissipation when he lived at Coulommes the second time would seem to be some confirmation of these assertions.

Note 18 Page 137

This date is taken from the issue of the *Figaro* for 10th June, 1924, where the particulars of Verlaine's military service papers are given.

Note 19 Page 154

Among them MM. Séché and Bertaut, in their work previously mentioned:

> The last-named (i.e. old Létinois), was a wily peasant. Without realising exactly the nature of the feeling these two young men (sic) had for one another, he saw only one thing, what a fine prey might be seized in Verlaine and his little fortune. One fine day the two went off together (Verlaine and Lucien) to London, leaving old Létinois there with the farm, who did not worry about a little thing like that, but sold the farm, which was in his name and put the proceeds in his pocket.

And that is how history is written!

Note 20 Page 179

The letters of March 10th and 21st are previously unpublished, I believe, and are a part of the fine Jacques Doucet collection; that of 29th September, 1888, to an unknown correspondent was published by M. Pierre Dufay (*La Connaissance*, November, 1920). That from Leon Deschamps to René Ghil is given by M. Armand Lods in *Les premières éditions de Paul Verlaine* (extract in the *Mercure de France*, October 15th, 1924).

Note 21 Page 185

Here, out of so many others, is one bill for lodgings and meals that Verlaine's heirs had to settle. It emanates from the Hotel de Montpellier. *Pension de famille et plat du jour*. Maison Bernard:

M. Verlaine came in on December 3rd, 1892. 18 rue des Cartes, room number 16, at sixteen francs a month.

Three months, December, January 1893, February and March	48.00 frs.
Meals and beverages in December	19.00 frs.
January, meals, ditto.	11.30 frs.
February	10.35 frs.
March 1893	9.05 frs.
	49.70 frs.
Room	48.00 frs.
	97.70 frs.

REFERENCES

The text of the poems quoted in translation in the text will be found in the definitive edition of Verlaine's works, in the volume and at the page given below.

OEUVRES COMPLÈTES } de PAUL VERLAINE.
& OEUVRES POSTHUMES } Albert Messein, 1925–6

The number of the volume is given in roman, the page in arabic, numerals, thus: Volume 1, page 119 . . . i, 119.

BOOK V

CHAPTER I

122   As the poem, *London Bridge*, has not been yet included in the *Oeuvres complètes* we give the text here:

Regarde ces flots noirs, ce grand fleuve de boue
Roulant tous les débris fangeux de la Cité:
Tu verras par moment briller une clarté,
Une paillette d'or où le soleil se joue.

Et si tu peux, regarde à présent dans mon coeur!
Peut-être y verras-tu quelque vague lumière;
C'est comme un souvenir de sa beauté première,
Et c'est assez, vois-tu, pour le rendre meilleur.

Car l'espoir est pareil au soleil qui se joue.
Tous deux ont le pouvoir de créer ces clartés:
Quelques rêves divins pour les coeurs dévastés
Et quelques reflets d'or pour les fleuves de boue!

INDEX